**Praise f**

Rachel Marie Martin has invited us to find joy, be brave, and now start a fire in our soul. Her writing is honest, open, and deeply insightful about the human condition. *Get Your Spark Back* starts as an ember and builds to an inspirational brushfire. Stop, drop, and roll into the nearest bookstore to grab a copy for yourself or someone you love.

— Pat Hazell, original writer of *Seinfeld*

Rachel Marie Martin's book is like holding up a mirror to your face that says, "You're worth the risk. So take it!" Reading this book, you'll relate through laughter and tears and be reminded that, no matter what age you are or what state in life you're in, it's never too late to follow your heart. You just have to take that first step and believe that by doing so you will have just created a spark that will start an amazing fire.

— Rebecca Lines, actor in *Cobra Kai* and
Marvel's *Falcon and the Winter Soldier*

Rachel Marie Martin is a bright light in the world and a voice of encouragement, hope, and comfort. I'm endlessly inspired by her vulnerable sharing and grateful that I've had the chance to learn from her hard-won wisdom.

— Lori Deschene, founder of Tiny Buddha

## Praise for *Mom Enough*

I can confidently say there are no words that make me breathe easier than the words of Rachel Marie Martin. No matter how long you've guilt-tripped yourself, neglected your needs, or abandoned your dreams, this compassionate guide offers real hope. Through relatable struggles and heartfelt honesty, Rachel shows us how to honor ourselves throughout our motherhood journey. Let *Mom Enough* bring peace to your soul and more of YOU to the brave story of your life.

—Rachel Macy Stafford, *New York Times*–bestselling author, speaker, and special education teacher

Rachel's words resonate—with the new mom, the tired mom, the single mom, the empty-nester and more. These letters articulate what so many women feel through the various seasons of motherhood. You will feel her heart as you read these letters and be reminded you aren't alone.

—Jenn Hamrick, founder of Story Social Media

Rachel Martin is a genius observer and storyteller of the human condition. Her writing reaches deep into the heart while allowing us to feel seen, heard, and soothed.

—Shonda Moralis, MSW, LCSW, coach, psychotherapist, and author of *Breathe, Mama, Breathe: 5-Minute Mindfulness for Busy Moms* and *Don't Forget to Breathe: 5-Minute Mindfulness for Busy Women*

# GET YOUR
# SPARK
# BACK

# GET YOUR
# SPARK
# BACK

## HOW TO FIND HAPPINESS
## AND REIGNITE YOUR LIFE

### RACHEL MARIE MARTIN

DEXTERITY
NASHVILLE

604 Magnolia Lane
Nashville, TN 37211

Printed in the United States of America.

First edition: 2024
10 9 8 7 6 5 4 3 2 1

ISBN: 978-1-962435-04-8 (Trade Paperback)
ISBN: 978-1-962435-05-5 (E-book)
ISBN: 978-1-962435-06-2 (Audiobook)

Publisher's Cataloging-in-Publication Data

Names: Martin, Rachel Marie, author.
Title: Get your spark back : how to find happiness and reignite your life / Rachel Marie Martin.
Description: Includes bibliographical references. | Nashville, TN: Dexterity, 2024.
Identifiers: ISBN: 978-1-962435-04-8 (paper) | 978-1-962435-05-5 (ebook) | 978-1-962435-06-2 (audio)
Subjects: LCSH Happiness. | Self-actualization (Psychology) | Change (Psychology) | Self-help. | BISAC SELF-HELP / Personal Growth / General | SELF-HELP / Motivational & Inspirational | SELF-HELP / Personal Growth / Happiness
Classification: LCC BF632 .M37 2024 | DDC 158--dc23

Cover design by twolineSTUDIO.
Interior design by PerfecType.

*For my family*

# CONTENTS

# CONTENTS

# PROLOGUE

Alice asks the cat: "Which road should I take?"
In reply, the cat says: "Where are you going?"
To that, Alice says: "I don't know."
"Then it doesn't matter which road you take,"
the cat says in response.
—*Alice in Wonderland*

I've never caught on fire.

I have been fascinated with fire since I was a little girl growing up in Minnesota. During my childhood, I was afraid of fire, probably due to the 1980s "Stop, Drop, and Roll" safety campaign. I knew exactly what to do to put the fire out and assumed that catching on fire wasn't a maybe thing; it was a *sure* thing. No one tells second graders during the fire safety lesson after math class that the probability of physically catching on fire is less than

1 percent. Second graders assume if you're teaching something, they need to learn and prepare for it.

Therefore, as a good second grader, I assumed catching on fire *would* happen.

It never did.

My younger self also assumed that life would emulate the sitcoms we watched at night. I grew up loving *The Cosby Show*, *Family Ties*, and *The Facts of Life*, where life's greatest problems could be resolved in twenty-two minutes once a week with a chuckle and a poignant life lesson. My youthful assumptions also meant I believed I'd finish college, get married, have a couple kids, own a nice house with a vegetable garden, and live with enough money for everything plus some vacations. Think of it as "the good-life assumption." The assumption? If you're an overall good person and follow the expected and prescribed steps, fill in the correct boxes, and don't make too much of a scene, then life will probably turn out okay.

Until it didn't . . .

I lost my spark.

It was in the weeds of life, deep in the unassumed realities of divorce, estranged kids, financial struggles, health issues, and a pandemic. I knew how to survive, how to take care of everyone and everything else, but in the quest to get out of the weeds, the fire of myself dimmed.

And then I caught on fire.

This fire was my soul, my true self, coming back to life. I was tired of stopping, of cutting myself short, of dropping out of the game of life. I wanted to play despite the messy path, wanted to find happiness, and wanted to cultivate purpose, so instead of rolling this fire out—*I stood up.*

I fought for my heart, my dreams, my mindset, my friendships, and my life.

Standing up allowed oxygen to rush into my soul.

My soul no longer was denied in the busy, lost in the past, or told to wait.

Instead, my happiness returned, my soul's fire reignited, and I went all in on my life.

This is my soul's journey.

# INTRODUCTION
## When You've Lost Your Spark

Fire has always held a level of magic, of mysticism, to me. I spent much of my childhood understanding how to put fire out but barely learned what it took to ignite it. I knew theoretically but didn't know practically how it worked. Throughout history, fire has held a critical role—a symbol of progress, safety, and advancement. And I knew the best way to describe a life filled with purpose was that of a soul on fire.

That's because I thought I lost my spark.

I'm guessing you resonate with that too. Maybe you remember the day when you wondered where your spark went. Maybe you feel like you've settled or are just watching life pass you by. Maybe you're on the other side of some really hard stories and you don't feel like you have the energy, direction, or drive to get your spark back. And maybe you feel like you are the only one with an ember waiting to be reignited.

Your soul's fire, the heart of all human experience, is the part of you that feels most alive, invigorated, grateful, and happy to be alive. It's also the part of our experience that can feel like it's being smothered, rolled out, or gone. But your spark is still there. It's just waiting for you to have the courage to say, "Today is the day I get it back."

It's so easy to neglect our souls while on life's journey. It's easy to settle, to think it's too late, to believe that the second half of life will mirror the first, to wait for clarity, and to watch life pass us by. It's also just as easy to think we're too much, too bright, and need to douse our identity. And all of that can make us wonder, *Where's my spark?*

Since the beginning of time, fire has been integral to our collective human experience. We can create it, control it, fuel it, and extinguish it. But, unlike physical fire, your soul's fire, as long as you're still breathing, doesn't go out. It may be small, hidden, the dimmest glow, or it may even feel lost altogether, but your soul is desperately waiting for you to spark life into it again.

*There is a fire within you.*

This is the fire of you living fully alive with all your potential. It is the fire of joy, laughter, adventure, happiness, bravery, advocacy, and courage. It is the fire of doing hard things, challenging the norm, reframing beliefs, trying new things, embracing happiness, and living with purpose. It is the fire of stepping into your story, being proud of your accomplishments, learning from your past, and living excited for what is to come. It is you, fully embracing life.

But life can throw challenges our way—devastating, unpredictable, course-altering ones—that can make our fire, our spark, feel smothered. Sometimes these things are out of our control, and sometimes we make choices that look like settling. And instead of remembering that we have the power to keep going, we start to wonder, *Is this really my life? What is the point? What is the meaning of life?* And *How do I find happiness again?*

I know because I've also felt the confusion in those same questions, and I've fought to be a soul-fire advocate. I've written since 2008 on my platform, *Finding Joy*, on the musings, insights, perplexities, frustrations, and flops. Over the years, I've shared raw, messy, beautiful, unexpected places with millions, and those readers have watched me quite literally take back my own life, create change, and find myself again. It's been an emotional journey with ups and downs, stalls and starts, a great deal of letting go, creating new paradigms, and, most recently, getting my soul's fire back.

## THE NEED TO REIGNITE

Around five years ago, I realized that although I had come through many challenges (divorce, moving, single parenting, financial hardship, creating a blended family), part of me still felt hollow, uninspired, and uncertain. In the hustle of solving problems, I had avoided addressing this internal ache. Then one day, in the middle of regular life (and not perfect timing either!), I began to wonder who I was now. I knew who I *had* been, but now? I wasn't so sure, and not being sure made me incredibly uncomfortable. In those days, I'd hear a shaky, "I don't know anymore."

I knew my external roles but had lost sight of the core of me. I knew how to show up for everyone else but had forgotten how to do the same for myself.

I knew I needed to reignite my soul.

In the beginning, I felt as if I was alone in the middle of the densest, foggiest, darkest forest. I couldn't see the way out, couldn't use the stars for direction, and couldn't rely on anyone but myself to take the first step. I'd tell my husband, Dan, and my friends how lost I felt, but often they couldn't see it. They could only see the external me—the mom, wife, and friend—who kept going, doing, and showing up. They couldn't see the ache in my soul to return to myself. My battle, my journey, was within.

I started taking steps without knowing if they were right or wrong. I trusted that each step would bring me closer to clarity and that if it didn't, I would be okay regardless. I told myself I'd rather move than do nothing. I wrestled with myself. I dealt with my beliefs on aging, midlife, legacy, purpose, my past, and what it means to live a good life.

In the wrestling, I realized that every day we are given two choices—do nothing or do something.

I chose to do something. And the act of *doing* is what reignited my soul.

Readers watched. Friends watched. Family watched. Neighbors watched. And as my fire began to grow, as I began to find my way, others began to ask me, "How do I get *my* spark back?"

That question is raw, vulnerable, brave, and revealing. It's never, "How do I get *a* spark?" but rather, "How do I get *my* spark *back*?" To get something back means to reclaim something you once had. If you've ever watched preschoolers play and one takes another's toys, the toddler without the toy has no problem grabbing the toy back. The presupposition in the word *back* is, "It's mine, I had it, I don't know where it is, but I want it back." Of course, we're not toddlers, but that's the level of energy you need to embody on this quest.

It is your spark, and you want it reignited. It is your soul's fire, and you want it back.

I'm proud of you for wanting it back. I'm proud that you have the courage to say, "Today is my start." And to believe that the ember of you is waiting. Trust me . . . it's just waiting for you.

The purpose of this journey is twofold: it's about finding your soul's fire and then, once found, tending to it so it continues to burn brightly. This book will help you identify and address your limits, your past, and mindsets that might be holding you back. It gives answers to the questions I ran into (and you've asked) along the way.

I need you to know this: I went on this journey during the most unchill and unlikely of times. I had just gotten remarried, bought a house, and was working at blending families—and then the pandemic hit. There is no right time to reignite your spark! If you're waiting for the perfect time to breathe life into your soul again, you could end up waiting your life away—and how deeply sad that would be. You must be willing, just as I was, to *do something* even if you can't see the path. Your soul deserves for you to take a step today.

*You are your number-one advocate on your life journey.* You must decide, "I am worth investing in me."

⋈ ✦ ⋈

The primary question I receive from followers and readers is, "How do I get my spark back?" And the primary comment I receive is, "Thank you for letting me know I'm not alone."

You are not alone, my friend. You aren't alone in dealing with struggles, tragedies, abandonment, and uncertainty. You aren't alone in hitting a midlife moment. You aren't alone if you wonder, *Is this it? Is this all there is to life?* You aren't alone if you feel small or that it's too late. You aren't alone if you just want to be happy again.

I believe in you.

I believe in your capabilities, your strength, your bravery, and your courage. I believe you can start and try. I believe you're tired of settling and you want vibrancy, that you want happiness and purpose. And I believe, deep down, that you know this about you too.

I want you to get your spark back. To go from looking for your spark to nurturing your soul's fire and living with purpose, happiness, and intention.

Your soul is waiting.

# HOW TO USE THIS BOOK
## Tending to the Embers

I'm so excited you've picked up this book and decided to go on this journey with me. That fire inside you may be just hot coals at the moment, but I promise the spark is there, just waiting to be ignited. Before we dive in, I'd like to share a few guidelines that I think will serve you well as you tend to the embers and begin to fan the flames of your spirit.

## BE WILLING TO WONDER

Getting your spark back will require some uncomfortable thinking. Humans tend to avoid the uncomfortable or look for reasons to get out of doing, thinking, or feeling the thing outside our comfort zone. Pay attention to those times when you think, *Nope. I can't do that*, and instead allow yourself the freedom to ask, *I wonder what might happen if I try?* Wondering is a lost art and is the daydreaming of possibilities. You are worth the gift of wondering.

## DEDICATE THE TIME

Have you observed the time and effort it takes to create fire? Unless you're Merlin the Magician or you have an instant soul spark lighter, this process takes time. Don't shortchange yourself by not allowing yourself time to think, to reframe, and to try new things. Remember: no one will set aside time for yourself except you.

## ALLOW DISCOMFORT

I've been a runner for seven years now. For the last three, running has been part of my soul journey. Don't worry, I'm not going to tell you that running is the way to find yourself (although I often use it as an analogy)! I will tell you this, though: running, for the most part, is *uncomfortable* for me. The "runner's high," that brief period of bliss or euphoria that comes after physical exertion? I've experienced it once, *maybe* twice. But I don't run for the high. I run because I know the threshold for my discomfort shifts and what once was uncomfortable becomes doable.

Change requires an element of discomfort. Rather than a sign to quit, discomfort is oftentimes an indicator of being on the right track.

## TAKE WHAT WORKS

Before we go any further, I want to give you permission to agree and disagree with what's to come. None of my words are hard and fast. Many of these principles have been learned from my own life experience and writing and with a tremendous amount of reading and research. But like my kids will remind you, I'm human. I make mistakes. And there is no one-size-fits-all. What works in my life might not be exactly what works for you. My solutions are meant to inspire you to uncover your solutions. No one shares the exact same starting place, histories, or mindsets.

This isn't about adopting my practices exactly but rather is about being inspired, wondering, and discovering your fire starters.

*The you five years
from now
needs you not to
give up on her
dreams.*

✴ ✦ ✴

Rachel Marie Martin
2019

# CHAPTER 1

# WHERE DO I START?

## Change Starts When
## You Make the Choice

One of my favorite children's books is *The Lorax* by Dr. Seuss. My childhood library book pile often included Seuss's books. I'd borrow *The Lorax* time and time again, even if I'd borrowed it weeks prior. In 2012, on what would have been Seuss's 108th birthday, *The Lorax* was made into a movie, one that I've seen at least a dozen times.

While the book's main premise is regarding environmentalism, some powerful life lessons are woven into the primary narrative. There are three main characters: the Once-ler, the Lorax, and the boy who visits him (since he's called Ted in the movie, I'll use that here). The story starts with Ted wandering into a desolate area to visit the Once-ler, a strange loner of a man. The Once-ler, after some insisting, tells Ted his story. The book alternates between present time and when the Once-ler met the Lorax many years prior.

The Once-ler, an ambitious entrepreneur, and the Lorax were at odds over a natural resource, Truffula trees. The Once-ler made a garment from the tufts of the trees and found a demand in the marketplace, which led to him chopping down the trees. The Lorax, the self-proclaimed speaker for the trees, was appalled and pleaded with the Once-ler, to no avail, to stop cutting down the trees. Year after year, the Lorax would beg him to stop, until in a dramatic moment, you see the very last Truffula tree chopped down. Then the Lorax flies off, leaving the Once-ler alone in a desolate world. The only thing the Lorax left behind was a pile of rocks with the word *unless* written on them.

By the time Ted enters the picture, the environment is crappy. The trees are gone, it's smoggy, and it seems too late to do anything. Yet he's curious about the Lorax's lore and treks out to the Once-ler to learn the story of where the Lorax once stood. The Once-ler describes in detail the events that went down and finally points to the Lorax's pile of rocks, with the word *unless* visible on them. In that moment, the Once-ler finally understands the meaning.

He throws Ted the last Truffula seed from his window and says, "Unless someone like you cares a whole awful lot, nothing is going to get better. It's not."[1]

*Unless someone like you cares.*

The Once-ler didn't tell Ted life was over and to quit because the world was bleak. He didn't tell him he was a victim of the past. He didn't tell him change would be easy. He didn't tell him to ignore the problems. He didn't tell Ted change would be fun. He didn't tell him that it wasn't his problem just because he didn't cause it. And he didn't tell him how to get the last seed to grow. He *only* told him to care "a whole awful lot." Not dip-your-toe-in care but all-in care.

You have the same mission, no matter your story. You need to care about your spark, your happiness, and your life's journey. Ted didn't chop down the trees or create the dark reality he was living in. How he got there didn't matter. What mattered was his decision to care, to take responsibility, for the rest of his story.

No matter what has happened to you, *you get to care enough to choose your response.* Your response, your mindset, your outlook—you are the only one in charge of those things. Ted could have decided that it was too much, that it was too late, that his impact wouldn't matter. Would we have read *The Lorax* to our kids if the solution at the end was defeat? Absolutely not. We read it because it represents the power of making one decision.

One decision—that's it. It's the decision to care.

You can decide to accept your intrinsic value and worth. You can take that seed of possibility found in you—no matter where you are on your timeline—and care for it. You can value yourself, and in valuing yourself, you'll see how blaming others and waiting for things to change doesn't result in anything.

When you value time, you will take that seed of opportunity and *plant it.*

It's your time. No more waiting for tomorrow. No more blaming the past. No more wondering if you can survive this journey. No more stalling. No more too-small limits.

Your time is now. It's time to start reigniting your life.

## WHY "WASTING" TIME ISN'T THE POINT

One of the greatest risks we take in life is not allowing ourselves to start.

As we get older, we often give ourselves less grace to figure things out. That's when procrastination's roar is loudest—with the fear that we won't be able to figure out who we are or what we want to do and will end up frittering away the present in a quest for an unknown and uncertain future. In other words, wasting time. Our definition for *wasting time* can also complicate matters.

Perhaps your second-grade teacher told you doodling was a time waster even though you loved to draw. Then instead of spending your free time doodling, you stopped and stared out the window. But then you were told that doing nothing was also a waste of time, so instead of daydreaming and coming up with ideas, you stopped allowing boredom and kept yourself busy with concrete, rewardable tasks like filling out another sheet of math facts you already mastered. Perhaps you were told to always put your time to good use, so the idea of making a theoretically time-wasting decision instantly gets thrown out. But were any of those activities time wasters? Or were you simply dreaming about the possibility of what could be?

Culture typically rewards visible, productive, measurable tasks as a good use of time. The definition of what is a "waste of time" is typically based on another person's opinion about what constitutes a good use of time. And that isn't the same for everyone.

Even now, I struggle to allow myself the freedom to experience the spaces that some might consider a waste of time. As a writer, I need to daydream, doodle, and wonder. It's hard to give myself permission because part of me still feels like these activities aren't productive. But sometimes productivity might *look* like wasting time. Sitting down to come up with dreams might not seem practical, but it is infinitely more productive than pushing through without direction.

With age also comes the pressure of time. I no longer feel as if I have all the time in the world and will jokingly ask if anyone can spare me an extra hour each day. But even if we magically upped our days to twenty-five hours, would we use that time to pursue our dreams, or fill the extra hour with busyness?

Time's acceleration is amplified when you witness time being cut short (or what we collectively deem as short). When my uncle Bob tragically died in his fifties, the consensus was that his life had been cut short. We mourned for what could have been and what he would miss. But when my kids' great-grandma Krusina died at 101 years old, most felt she had lived a good, long life. Her funeral, while still sad, felt like more of a celebration of a long life lived.

Death isn't the only way the pressure of time awakens. Maybe you're like me and are close to the half-century mark and wonder who you are and what to do next. Perhaps the dreams you thought you would have accomplished by now haven't been touched, let alone remembered. Maybe you're dealing with a health scare, and instead of the next year being devoted to travel, you'll be in and out of the clinic. Maybe you received unexpected news that rocked your awareness. Maybe you're dealing with financial issues that have been creating extra anxiousness and work. Maybe you are busy with jam-packed school schedules and feel like you don't have a minute to catch up or add anything new. Those maybes amplify time's pressure.

I don't need to hammer in the pressure of time, because I know you get it.

You *get* that time is moving.

You *get* that you have one shot at this earthly life.

You *get* that you should use your time wisely.

You *get* that time is finite.

So let me ask you this: Even though you understand time, do you *live* like you understand it?

My kids get the rule of no dirty clothes left on the floor. If I come in a room, see clothes strewn to kingdom come, and remind them of the rule, they'll probably say, "I know. I know." Even though they're outwardly acknowledging the rule, their actions aren't in line. Or they might say, "I forgot," which tells me the rule didn't matter too much to them. They might even say,

"I was too busy." In that case, the rule was overtaken by something else.

You can't *get* the gift of time and do nothing, forget about it, or be too busy. If you understand the urgency of time, why is it so hard to stay motivated? Why is it easier to say, "I'll start next month," but then default, forget, or find something else to do? Why does it take amplifiers and shake-ups to wake us up?

I think it's because life, at times, can feel pointless.

I feel like I might be struck by lightning for writing those words! They feel dangerous, like they shouldn't be said aloud, like admitting I sometimes feel this way means I might be opening Pandora's box. Maybe I am opening the box of unspoken thoughts and, in the opening, I'm simply letting light into a dark room of unsaid fears: life *can* feel pointless, and it can also feel like time is being wasted.

Is it possible that life feels pointless *when* time is actually wasted—and that our definition of *wasting time* may have been wrong all along? Is it also possible that it feels pointless when we've lost direction or our spark dims?

Wasting time doesn't mean resting, taking a vacation, or daydreaming. It doesn't mean you're wrong for sitting on the porch and watching the birds or lying under a tree with a good book. Cuddling up with your loved ones in front of a movie isn't a waste of time. Investing in yourself and your family, doing things that make you happy, is a beautiful, noble, and great use of time.

So what does it actually mean to *waste time*? Wasting time means you default on your story, you put off finding your spark, you ignore responsibility, and you accept feeling lost versus finding your way out.

And if we clarify the definition of *wasting time*, I believe that asking, "What is the point?" is actually a *good* thing. It's a needed life-check question. When you ask, you create space for an honest conversation about your daily life. You open the door to identify what matters to you and why you might feel lost.

You are never wasting time when you begin to pay attention to the whispers of your soul.

## *YOU* ARE THE POINT

Between every stimulus is a millisecond, a gap, when the power of the response is in your hands. You get to choose. Yes, there are times when the stimulus is powerful and you have to respond immediately (like when you're about to be T-boned in an intersection). But there are a million other moments and micro-decisions when you don't have to just react.

You can choose.

So then, when the question, "What is the point?" creeps in, you don't have to feel guilty, fearful, anxious, dumb, worried, or alone.

You can answer, "I am the point."

> Sometimes when I'm running and I'm super tired, I think back to a contestant on America's Got Talent named Nightbirde. She was young and had stage 4 cancer, and despite her diagnosis, she came to sing her song titled "It's OK." She immediately caught the hearts of all the judges and the world.[2] Several months after her song went to the top of iTunes, she died. When I'm tired and wondering, What is the point to running? I keep going because she reminded me of the gift in getting to keep going.

In addition to not wasting time, I'm betting you were taught from a young age to have a clear purpose to the things you do. Do your homework, and you'll get a good grade on the test. Practice free throws, and you'll have a great free throw percentage. Train for a 5K, and you'll cross the finish line as they call your name. Work hard at the mid-level job, and one day you'll become the boss. Wash your face to prevent acne. Save your money so you'll have enough to retire. Clean the Rice Krispies off the bowl so they don't become superglue.

Do something, and an outcome is guaranteed.

When my daughter Chloe was a little girl, she decided to remove what I thought were unremovable wooden wheels off a model car. Her wheel-removing ability has remained one of our family's greatest mysteries. When she showed me the wheels and asked me to put them back on, I couldn't figure out how to put them on or how she got them off in the first place. Finally, I asked her why she did it (remember—we're always looking for the point of something), and my almost four-year-old simply said, "I do it."

She just did it.

Knowing the point to our actions isn't a negative. Knowing the point can help us make sound, safe, wise decisions. Knowing the point can also help us push through hard times or challenges. But there are other times when our actions and words might feel pointless.

If my kids never learned to put their clothes in the hamper and I kept telling them day after day, I might begin to wonder, *What's the point?* Sometimes life can make us feel like a hamster running on a wheel, putting in tons of effort but going nowhere. And that's when most of us wrestle with the point of things.

The secret to life, the deep "What's the point?" answer, has perplexed humans since the dawn of time. Philosophers philosophize (I've been waiting to use that word) and write many books—only to leave us with the same question: "What's the meaning of life?" Or said in more contemporary words and less philosophically, "What's the point?"

Is it to be a good person? To start a charity? To help those in need? Is it to make a bunch of money? To leave a legacy? To create social change? To have an amazing garden? To travel? To write books? To raise good kids? To be happy?

What is the point?

Life doesn't have a clearly defined "if you do A, it will lead to B, which will then guarantee C" outcome. Life is full of twists and turns and unexpected events, and even though we did A and B, we may find ourselves in a life that looks like J. Or it's C and we're unhappy and feel guilt over not being happy because we thought the point was to get to C and C isn't what we expected.

In other words: it's complicated.

But what if the question we're asking is inherently flawed? What if it isn't a global "What is the meaning of all life?" Perhaps the question isn't the meaning of life but rather, "What is the meaning of *your* life?"

*Your* life. Not the life your parents hoped for you. Not the life you were told was the right life. Not the life you see your friends living. Not the Instagram influencer's life. Not the "if you do A and B, you will get to C" life. But your unique, individual life. After all, *you are the only you* in existence. You're it. As cliché as it sounds, let that sink in a bit.

You. Are. It.

The hands holding this book or ears listening to the words are unique to you. Your eyes, your fingerprints, your heart, your dreams, your spark, your timeline. Your life has meaning not because of the things that you do, accomplish, finish, worry about, complete, change—but simply because you are you.

You get to set your bar, your standard, your expectation of living *for you*. You get to determine how you use your time and if you waste time waiting or spend it living. You get to decide your point.

## WHEN THE END IS JUST A BEND

While I was writing this book my second son, Caleb, was finishing his senior year in high school. Between edits, it's been six months of FAFSA college financial aid forms, graduation gown orders, college visits, and yearbook projects. If you were to talk with him about what he wants to study, he might hesitate, because despite knowing he's attending college, he doesn't know his why. I've told him that he'll figure it out as he walks through the experience. Instead of saying, "I don't know," I told him to reply with, "I'm excited to figure it out."

Most high school seniors are asked to share their hopes and dreams for the yearbook. They'll write about finishing college, how the sky's the limit, and how they're going to wholeheartedly chase their dreams. I'm pretty sure no inspirational yearbook quotes say, "When I'm forty, I want to go through a nasty divorce." No one is sharing hopeful words about dealing with death, illness, financial ruin, betrayal, or any of the other hard but often unspoken chapters a person might walk through. Because no one plans for these unspoken realities, when we hit those points in life, we can feel a bit ripped off by the unfair twist in the story. It's often at that moment when the "What's the point?" question is the loudest.

Hard experiences were never part of our original life plot—especially not when were told that the point was to get a good job, settle down, have a family, make money, and retire.

Difficult moments often blindside us, and we find ourselves in an environment we absolutely could not have predicted and certainly wouldn't have chosen. And in that challenging environment, the Once-ler is telling us we need not only to care but also to take action to change things. Truthfully, it can be hard to care when the path ahead is foggy or daunting. It's exceptionally hard to care when you've been knocked down. And if you've lived life with a ridiculous number of knockdowns, caring can feel not only impossible but also downright risky.

If you get knocked down enough times, you might decide it's safer not to care—because if you care, you might get hurt. You might just accept the "it is what it is" philosophy to life. While this might seem like a safe approach, like a way to protect your heart, not caring and not acting, as time passes, will hurt you worse. The choice to not care can lead to dashed hopes, words unspoken, and regrets. Not caring takes us right back to the question, "What is the point?"

In 2018, I published my first book, *The Brave Art of Motherhood*. Several months before it hit the shelves, postdivorce drama hit my house (my separation was in 2013, but I was still dealing with fallout five years later). A couple years after my divorce in December 2016, I moved from Minneapolis to Nashville in hopes of building a better life for myself and the kids. But that meant making the very challenging decision to move them from their biological father. Despite his lack of involvement in their lives, it was still one of those times in life when the right answer was wrought with complications. As a result, in July 2018, my fifteen-year-old son, Brennan, decided to no longer live in Nashville and to stay with his dad in Minneapolis.

Divorce is complicated. Even though my story had me untethering myself from a dysfunctional and unhealthy marriage, my kids' story had their family splitting apart. Just like we look for a point in circumstances or events, we also often look for someone to blame. For many years, I took the brunt of my kids' anger, hurt, and confusion. Even though I knew I had made the right decision in moving, there still was fallout, most of which fell on me.

Brennan and I had been struggling ever since the move, and the tension between us was palpable that summer. I didn't know what to do to solve the stress, but I did know I desperately wanted him happy again. That July, I drove the kids back to Minnesota for a week at the cabin with my family and then a week with their dad (this is the only time they see him each year). When it was time to drive back to my home in Nashville, Brennan asked for two more weeks with his dad. I pleaded for him to come back with us, but after an hour I realized my fighting was in vain, so I reluctantly agreed to the two weeks.

Remember how I wanted him to find happiness? Since I was at my wit's end, since I'd tried everything I felt I could (counseling, mentors, etc.), and despite the angst of letting him stay, part of me was hopeful that he could heal. After a tearful, gut-wrenching goodbye, I went inside and immediately bought him a one-way ticket back to Tennessee. For two weeks it was radio silence, and my mom heart fretted and worried about him. Then, the day before he was to fly back, I received a text from his dad telling me, "Brennan is staying here with me."

I tried to fight it, but there was no budging. If Brennan was with me, even with our tension, I knew we'd focus on school, getting a driver's license, a job, mental health, and healthy meals. With him gone, I didn't know if any of these things would happen. I was between a rock and hard place and felt as if I was the worst mom in the world, a failure.

*How could this have happened?*

I never planned for divorce, and I certainly didn't plan for my fifteen-year-old son to live a thousand miles from my home. I also didn't plan for the angst of trying to co-parent with someone who wasn't on the same page as me. I was stuck. School was starting in two days, and I knew that even if I went there to get him, he wouldn't return with me. There was just too much baggage between us.

This wasn't my plan for life. This wasn't my plan for his life. This wasn't his plan for his life. This wasn't the plan. Ever.

It wasn't my plan to go several years with us barely communicating. It wasn't my plan to hear about how he was struggling but not be able to help. It wasn't my plan to have a gap in my other kids' lives. It wasn't my plan to watch my other kids struggle with fears that they didn't really matter to Brennan or their dad. It wasn't my plan to worry that my other kids would leave me. None of this was my plan.

I was angry. Mad. Misunderstood. Hurt. Devastated. Crushed. Guilt-ridden. Embarrassed. Ashamed. Worried. Beaten down.

On that muggy July evening when I got the text that Brennan was staying in Minnesota, I wept. Where was the joy? What was the point? What did I do wrong? As I cried, I wrote, and in the rawness these words were penned: *"Sometimes you have to let go of the picture of what you thought life would be like and learn to find joy in the story you are actually living."*

I shared the quote on my Finding Joy Facebook page, and those heartfelt words have now been shared over thirty million times. I didn't share at the time the story behind the words, but others showed up and responded with genuine kindness. I realized I wasn't alone; I wasn't the only one living a lemonade life story. I wasn't the only one determined to keep trying despite being in the middle of a life not going according to plan. I knew I couldn't stop, couldn't cash in my chips, couldn't fold my cards, couldn't quit—because the moment I felt like I didn't matter was when I heard my other kids saying, "Where's Mom?"

They needed me.

I'm sure they wanted a snack or they needed me to settle whose turn it was on the Xbox. The why was irrelevant. I knew I had to keep going, despite life's abrupt turn. I didn't see it then, but I do now—it wasn't the end, just a bend.

My kids needed me to be their rock. They needed me to be willing to find happiness amid an unplanned story. They needed me to fight for my story and, in that fight, their story. And more than that, *I* needed me. I needed me to be willing to navigate an uncharted path. I needed me to be willing to deal with the baggage. I needed me to be willing to live this life with purpose.

I needed to find happiness within.

It can be easy to look at others' lives and forget the complexity of their stories. Even though we *know* there is always more going on, we often still compare another's snapshot to our entire story. We see the social media update, and even though we *know* it's a highlight reel, we still compare it to our *real* reel. Our real lives are messy and full of non-yearbook-worthy moments that don't make it to Facebook, Instagram, or Christmas card letters. If we aren't careful, we can start to judge our real against a faux and filtered reel.

## THE PATH OUT OF THE SHADOWS

About four months after my son left, I was nervously waiting in the wings at the *Today* show. I was the featured guest for a segment about women reclaiming their financial story. My publicist turned to me and remarked, "This is an amazing day! Let's take a picture of you with the 'Today Is November 9' behind you. You need to remember this moment!" (the *Today* show has a large letterboard with "Today Is" and then the date on their set.)

I looked at the date and choked up. I knew I couldn't cry (television makeup), but that date broke me inside. You see, November 9 is Brennan's birthday. The son with whom I was barely speaking. The son I birthed, held when he had a bad dream, walked into school with, helped with his homework, sat in doctors' offices with, waited for the bus for. The son I saw every single day . . . until I didn't.

The high of this career moment coupled with the low of my familial pain was intense. It was the highest of highs and the lowest of lows smashed together into a moment of pure humanness.

I looked up at the date again, forced a smile, and took the picture.

Several days later, I shared that picture on Instagram alongside words about how the image you see isn't always the reality. I finally shared the *why* behind the viral quote, that I was living with estrangement as part of my story. I shared that it was Brennan's birthday and how gutted I was even though the world might only see an author who finally had her big break. I shared about how so often the real act of bravery and courage is how we keep going amid these painful moments. I shared about how we need to have grace for those around us and remember that often they, too, are living unexpected and maybe painful chapters.

We all have these shadow chapters in life.

Sometimes these shadow chapters resolve (my son moved back to Nashville a year ago, and with a lot of dedicated work, years of working hard to reconcile, many tears shed and moments of forgiveness, we now have a great relationship), or sometimes you continue to carry them with you. If I had written this book two years ago, we wouldn't have been to the point of resolution. I'd be at the part where I had to realize that I was still a good mom, that I mattered, even when the relationship wasn't perfect and that showing up for him didn't look like I imagined. And even if the shadow chapters resolve, you may still feel sadness about what was lost. I still mourn the five years he and I were apart.

Both Brennan and I did the best we could in the moment. There isn't a guidebook for most life events, and even if there was, no two events are the same. When we're in the middle of big life events, in the angst of struggle, we forget that doing our best often feels disjointed and unplanned. At times, doing our best and caring may mean doing hard things that others might not understand or might judge. You might even struggle to reconcile some of these choices. I want to assure you that those boundaries, those choices that feel painful in the moment, might actually be the path toward healing.

The path to healing is rarely visible from the start; often it is foggy, scattered with obstacles, and filled with highs and lows. All you're responsible for on your path is *your best at the time*. When you look back on these shadow seasons, you can't superimpose the you of now on the you of then. The you of now has learned, grown, and gained insight. Instead of harshly judging the earlier you, give yourself grace.

We each have our own timeline—mixed with the universe's timeline. Healing and reconciliation don't always cross at the same moment, and part of letting go and moving on involves hope and patience as you wait for moments when timelines intersect. I couldn't force Brennan's journey, just like you can't force yours.

Even though I felt like a bad mom during that season of separation, I was still being his mom. Loving him, waiting for him, praying for him, and showing up the best I could. It wasn't perfect, for sure, but I didn't quit. Even in the shadow place of my life.

None of us gets through life without shadow chapters. And they're hard. They can leave you feeling like you aren't enough, like you don't matter, like you screwed up, like you're not lovable, and so forth. During this shadow season in my life, people could tell me I was a good mom and doing my best, but I still had to wrestle with the shadow's residue.

That residue will cloud your view of the present and the future. Imagine driving with a windshield covered in grime. Instead of cleaning it, you grow accustomed to it. But if someone else got in the car, they might say, "Why don't you clean your windshield?" At some point, you became used to the obscured view.

That's residue.

The residue in our lives is the emotions, labels, and baggage we carry that potentially define our actions in the present. The residue is patterns of thinking that might no longer be for our benefit.

Unless you decide to clean up that residue, like finally cleaning your dirty windshield, your outlook will be limited as well. The antidote to the residue in life isn't to avoid it or to accept it; the antidote mirrors the Lorax's words—you have to care and you have to take action.

> Unless you decide to care, nothing will change.
> Unless you decide to forgive, you will carry hurt.
> Unless you decide to try, you won't start.
> Unless you decide to pivot, you won't move.
> Unless you decide to be brave, you will be fearful.
> Unless you decide to risk, you will stay small.
> Unless you decide to challenge, you will live within your limits.

Take a deep breath, gather your courage, and examine the residue in your life. It doesn't matter how it got there. You have the power to deal with it now. As we journey through this book, you will uncover residue—areas where you've settled, limits you've allowed regarding your potential, improper beliefs about time and money, and presuppositions you've made about your strength. And as you deal with this residue and come to a place of truth, it will be you who is cleaning your windshield and revealing a clear vision for the future.

*Unless* doesn't mean you need to have all the answers. *Unless* means you're willing to try to get your spark back, to rediscover happiness, and to reignite your story.

## FIRE STARTERS

+ **Find the step before the starting line.** You don't start a run once you hit the trail. The run starts the moment you put on your shoes. Likewise, in life, the first step in any change is to figure out the step *before* what seems like the first step. Say you're going to take a Pure Barre class. If you drive there, you'll more than likely walk in. The first step isn't to take the class; the first step is to leave the house for class. Find the step *before* the beginning, and nurture that space. This might be putting your shoes in front of the door or having a friend you meet at class.

+ **Clear the residue in your life.** Next time you turn on your windshield wipers, use that as a self-check. When we uncover fear, we often realize there's a layer *beneath* the fear. I like to then "turn on the wipers" and attempt to figure out what's behind that fear. Instead of being annoyed at what we find behind the residue, this is the time to redirect—you will survive it if you mess up, mistakes are part of the process, and seeing clearly leads to peace and a solution. Seeing the residue is a powerful first step in igniting your spark. When we don't deal with residue, it is like trying to light damp wood. Make the residue self-check a normal part of your week.

+ **Embrace vulnerability—with safety.** For many years, I felt too vulnerable to be vulnerable, as if I was the only one who had shadow chapters in my story. This thinking kept me isolated and hindered true connection. When I started to open up and share, like I did about my estrangement, others saw safety to open up and be vulnerable as well. Within this rawness, the power of caring, community, and change emerged. Being vulnerable doesn't mean you have to dump everything on your friends at once; it might be as simple as saying, "I need a friend." Being vulnerable also means letting yourself be vulnerable with yourself. That looks like dealing with hard stuff, giving yourself grace, and daring to take action.

# CHAPTER 2

# WHAT IS MY FIRST STEP?

## When Someday Becomes Now

*Grab a torch. Light it. Fire represents your life.*
—Jeff Probst, host of *Survivor*

The reality show *Survivor* has been on CBS for more than twenty years. I confess that I have watched every single season (and some of them twice). I can tell you the greatest villains, the underdogs, the best strategists, where the most challenging seasons were filmed, how the game moved from the classic era to the new era, and why fans have a love-hate relationship with their now seemingly permanent Fiji location.

Now, in case you aren't an extreme *Survivor* fan, let me set up the premise: Gather some strangers, put them on a deserted island, give them limited supplies, make them compete in challenges to earn more supplies and food, and then every couple days, have them vote out a teammate they just spent time building a relationship with. Toward the end of the season, voted-out contestants become part of a jury. This jury of backstabbed, blindsided, and often frustrated former contestants then decides which of the remaining three contestants will be awarded the million-dollar prize.

*Survivor* requires social prowess, mental stamina, and physical endurance while subsisting on limited sleep, little food, and zero privacy. You live in a makeshift camp surrounded by strangers who may be your new best friend or be totally untrustworthy. Oh, and cameras are recording your every move, which you've agreed can be edited and shown on national television. Sounds perfect, right?

It's epic. And revealing.

At the time of this writing, *Survivor* has been on for forty-six seasons. It's estimated that around 25,000 people apply each season for a chance to compete (more than 1.1 million individuals have submitted videos and questionnaires for this chance to put themselves to the ultimate test). The people who make it? They are normal people like you and me and our neighbors and the gal at church and the dude in front of you at Starbucks (or your barista at Starbucks). There is no difference between the contestants and the viewers except that the contestants applied. The fan favorites are often the underdogs, the ones who admit their fears or how they're tired of settling, of their self-imposed limits, of caring what others think, and as a result they put themselves in the most uncomfortable of situations.

Going on a reality show like *Survivor* is a chosen life shake-up.

Life is full of shake-up moments, some chosen like *Survivor*, some unexpected, and some that emerge as a slow realization, like the dreaded midlife crisis. There's no getting through life without the shake-ups. They either ignite your spark or threaten to snuff it out. And although they aren't what keep your soul's fire burning, some shake-ups do have the power to make you realize that you're coasting, that you're waiting on some magic thing to get your spark back, or that you've settled.

I know, even with the fears, that you want your spark back. I'm also guessing that, like me and so many others, you want to feel alive, vibrant, and full of vitality, but you aren't exactly sure of the steps to get there. You want the shake-up to have meaning, to matter—and for you to emerge a better version of you.

You may even wonder if it's still possible for you to find your spark. I'm here to assure you that you can—even if you're not sure of the how.

Your spark still exists. Ultimately, it doesn't matter how you got to this place; it only matters what you do now.

## FIRE REPRESENTS YOUR LIFE

The game of *Survivor* consists of not only camp dynamics but also physical challenges that require teamwork, smarts, and endurance. One tribe wins; one loses. During the last fifteen minutes of every episode, the losing tribe gathers to vote out one member. As the tribe members sit on rough-hewn benches with a roaring fire between them and the host, Jeff Probst questions them about camp life and personal issues while attempting to glean information on who might be voted out. The conversation can be raw, truth-uncovering, and volatile because Probst doesn't leave questions unanswered—he pushes each person to deal with their own demons, stereotypes, assumptions, and perceived flaws. Over the years, he has created space for issues that often aren't discussed, and as a result *Survivor* has been a platform for social change.

Before the fireside chat begins, Probst asks each participant to dip their torch into the fire as he says the now infamous words, "In this game, fire represents your life."

Can we pause and acknowledge the brilliance of those words? He doesn't say that fire represents life but rather fire represents *your* life. If your torch is lit, you're still in the game, you still have choices, you still have opportunities. And this applies to you and me too. The ember burning inside you is still there, waiting, reminding you that you're still in the game.

You may feel content, but perhaps your internal fire is dim. Remember, your fire is the core of you, the part of you that lights up at a concert when violins play in perfect harmony or that wakes up excited about the day in front of you. It's the part of you that feels deeply. It's the part that is the warrior, the believer, the dreamer, the doer, the giver, the lover, the caregiver, the friend, the runner, the fighter, the writer, the poet, the dancer, the knitter, the baker, the thinker. It's the you who has survived to this point, the you who didn't know if she had the answers but still made it through, and the you who realizes how important her spark is in life.

Your internal spark may be flickering, but it is not snuffed out. If there is breath in your lungs, you have the capacity to reignite you. That's part of why I love *Survivor*—it's a group of individuals who looked for adventure, believed in their abilities, decided enough was enough, and put themselves on the line.

At some point, they had to decide to apply. The first step wasn't going to the website and looking at the requirements. The first step was daring to think, *Should I do this?* and then instead of listening to every single reason why they shouldn't, proceeding anyway. That meant writing down their information, recording a video (probably rerecording and re-rerecording a video). It meant interviews and waiting and hoping. It meant having moments of *What in the world am I thinking?* Despite the doubts and the fears, each person has gone through the process of fighting for their iconic torch to be dipped in fire.

It meant interrupting their lives. It meant making their someday *today*.

I know you've got some of those somedays too.

*Someday I'll learn to play piano.*
*Someday I'll take that painting class.*
*Someday I'll start running.*
*Someday I'll learn to swim.*
*Someday I'll change my finances.*
*Someday I'll speak up.*
*Someday I'll find joy.*
*Someday I'll laugh.*

*Someday I'll start that business.*
*Someday I'll make new friends.*
*Someday I'll volunteer.*
*Someday I'll go to Italy.*
*Someday I'll visit my family.*
*Someday I'll see a counselor.*
*Someday I'll invest in myself.*
*Someday I'll get my spark back.*

No one on *Survivor* talks about how they took the risk so they could find their *partner's* spark or their *friend's* spark. *Survivor* is a journey of self-discovery in real time. Don't worry. I'm not asking you to apply for *Survivor!* But I am asking you to apply for your life again. With the gusto, all-in attitude, and determination of one of those contestants.

What would you tell the producers of the life you're looking for? What would you say on your submission video? Are you looking to find happiness? Deal with your past? Find courage? Forgive? Are you hoping to discover what you really want to do? To find peace? To be brave? Are you longing to connect with your soul again?

I want to encourage you to do more than ask the questions; I want you to answer them. Maybe you want to learn to overcome your fears. Is there a specific fear?

Why do you have this fear? Do you know its origin story? What does life look like with the fear? What might it look like without the fear? Are you afraid to let go of the fear? How would you feel without the fear?

These questions aren't meant to intimidate but to provide a glimpse into your soul. Our brains can be full of distracting chatter that keeps us from hearing or seeking out our truth. When you ask the questions, you also pause the chatter. Because the questions laser in on your truth, pay attention to your responses, and don't immediately dismiss them if they're uncomfortable. Allow yourself to simply wonder about the answers you hear. Wondering doesn't mean you agree or disagree; wondering is an inquisitive brainstorm session. Wondering removes the pressure of needing to understand immediately and cultivates curiosity. Curiosity doesn't judge but rather wants to learn, to discover, and ultimately to bring clarity and the "aha" revelations.

You can use a similar framework of questions for any area—fears, dreams, goals—you'd like to pursue. I encourage you to write them down and to spend some time pondering your answers. Think of it like peeling back the layers of an onion: there are many layers before you get to the center. Very often, the initial questions won't give you your final answer, but if you sit with the questions and continue to contemplate the answers, eventually you will get to the center of what you're seeking.

## THE PROMISE OF SOMEDAY

Have there been times in your life when you've told yourself that someday you'll take the risk, try the new thing, or take care of yourself? Did the list of someday questions make you uneasy or illuminate areas where you, too, have used the hollow promise of someday to keep yourself from doing? We are pretty darn good at lying to our brain with the promise of someday. I liken it to taking an Advil to dull the pain of a broken ankle but never actually fixing the ankle. You might be able to walk around, but you're not going to move at the speed you could. Other people might even see you limping and call you out on it. Instead of taking care of it, you deflect the attention with a hollow, "Yep, I need to do something!" as you continue to deal with it. Eventually, no matter how you deny it, push it off, ignore it, or tough it out, your broken ankle will catch up to you.

Several years ago, in a seemingly chill period of life, my own spark was flickering faintly. I was stuck in the busy, in being a good mom, wife, stepmom, daughter, writer, and neighbor. While in this busy season, caring for everyone else, managing schedules and stuff, I had put myself on the back burner. Logically, I knew I needed to nurture my spark, and I kept making empty promises to myself ("I'll spend some time focusing on my creativity, my spirit, what makes my soul sing"), but unlike how I kept my promises to everyone else, I didn't do a great job of keeping it for myself. I was so frustrated—frustrated that I kept telling myself I would take the time to nurture my spirit but then flaking out. Again. I was a master at keeping my word to everyone except myself.

At some point, I realized I had it muddled. Even though I knew I needed to take care of myself, I still felt it was my job as mom, friend, and partner to put everyone else first. I'd feel guilty for taking time for myself. The guilt would cloak itself in thoughts like, *If only you were a better mom, you'd be able to handle everything* and *take care of your needs.*

Yes, there are times when life is about caring and giving of yourself for others. But it isn't sustainable if you burn out in the taking care of everyone and everything else. That's like needing to drive forty-two miles and seeing that the gas gauge says you have only twenty-eight miles' worth of gas left—and trying to push through anyway, hoping you'll make it. Would you tell yourself that if you try really hard, you'll have enough gas?

Absolutely not. You'd stop, fill up the tank, and proceed on—without guilt.

Taking time for yourself is not an extra; it's an essential. I had been so focused on fixing my life—solving my finances, healing from divorce, moving my family, starting over—that I forgot about the internal. I forgot about the need to take time for my heart, my soul, too.

You can fix all the externals and still be dealing with internal carryover (residue).

In the summer of 2020, in the middle of the Covid years, when many of the external issues (finances, moving, remarriage) in my life were resolved or addressed, I realized that my soul was still so anxious and unsettled. There was a gnawing internal ache, and the question *Who am I now?* was on repeat. For so many years, I was the woman clawing out of challenges, and now that I was in the next phase, I didn't know what lit me up anymore.

The pandemic years cleared my schedule and allowed for most tasks and projects to be completed. All of a sudden, I couldn't escape myself or use "being busy" as a way to avoid dealing with my own soul. There wasn't a list of tasks to distract—it was just me finally getting a moment to pause and realizing that I didn't really know who I was anymore. It was my responsibility to figure out the next step.

I had grown tired of telling everyone else *yes* but telling myself *someday*. I realized I was worthy of my yes today. And you are too.

## FIGHT FOR YOUR STORY

Have you ever wondered why you lost your spark?

For a moment, let's stop asking why. Instead of basing future actions on the why of the past, let's try basing them on the why of the future. It's not why you lost your spark but *why you want your spark back*. Why does your spark matter to you? How will your future change if your spark is reignited?

Rather than dissecting the past, your future self needs you to go all in *now*, to fight for your story, to let go of the past, to fuel your soul, and to learn to love the writer of your story—you. You may have messed up, life may have thrown some curveballs, you may feel as if you're in too deep and don't have the answers, but you are still worthy of a beautiful, wonderful, purpose-filled life. When you live knowing you are worthy and mindful of the reason you want your spark back, you will move from watching life to doing life.

Most *Survivor* contestants fight hard, strategize, and compete so their torch won't be snuffed by Probst.

They'll jump in the ocean, solve puzzles while one hand is tied behind their back, and stand for hours under the scorching sun. They'll sleep on bamboo, endure body-covering insect bites, and eat meager rations of rice.

Is it about the million-dollar prize? Or is it about the experience? Of course, the prize money is a draw, but for most contestants, they are simply honored to play. In fact, when contestants quit, there is a general feeling of frustration because everyone knows that 24,982 people would have jumped at a chance to make it past the screening round. The experience is what the players make of it. Do they fold? Do they endure? Do they smile through the discomfort?

Endurance takes mental discipline and the ability to let go of the need to be perfect. You can't go into this reignition process trying to look or act like you have all the perfect answers. This raw human experience requires a stripping away of the labels, fears, expectations, and presuppositions we may have deemed unbreakable.

When you dare to examine your beliefs and question, "Why do I believe this to be true?" you unlock your life. Vulnerability creates authenticity. Authenticity creates truth. Truth creates hope. Hope creates potential. Potential creates action. Each contestant, in their dare to be vulnerable, ended up creating a domino effect of action and realization in their lives. The same is true for your life. When you are vulnerable with yourself you will create action.

Vulnerability means letting go of it being the right time or you making a fool out of yourself. Vulnerability places your heart, your soul, first. Are you really making a fool out of yourself by fighting for you?

If you want someday to matter, you need to stop running on empty, circling, stalling, avoiding, or whatever tactic you've employed in life to keep you afloat but not moving. You, and only you, are the only one who can decide to change the status of your someday to today.

Living all in is all about action and no longer placating your soul with *someday*.

It's your birthright to live fully alive. We just forget, we lose it, or we're terrified of moving forward. Your six-year-old self probably had no problem belting out songs. She didn't care what others thought or if she was too much— she sang because she loved to sing. My niece, June, will sing "Let It Go" into her karaoke mic as loud as she can because she has not let the world tell her to tone it down. She sings because she loves to sing. She's not worried *about what others think—she's singing because no one has told her not to sing and she knows, in her heart, that she's worthy of singing loud.*

*If you ask little kids what they want to be when they grow up, their answers reveal only possibilities, not settling. They'll tell you they want to be astronauts, ballerinas, teachers, or the president. At some point, life tells them that the moon is too far, dancing is for dreamers, teachers don't get paid enough, and the presidential office is too big a dream.*

*Life teaches them to be practical, to get a safe job, and to tuck those dreams down even further than someday—those dreams were just the follies of youth. Now instead of climbing Everest, we're hoping to go to Disney or get a couple days off extra to just rest. But were the dreams truly foolish?*

## WHEN HARD LEADS TO HAPPY

My father-in-law, Dave, served in the United States Air Force for twenty years. In 1973, five weeks after my husband, Dan, was born, Dave was sent to Greece for a year, guarding planes and living in less than stellar conditions. His wife, Mary, moved from the Air Force base in Wyoming to Dave's parents' home in Ohio. For Dan's first year of life, his mother was not only living in the newborn fog; she was doing it with her husband across the Atlantic and in her in-laws' home.

The only communication Dave and Mary had was handwritten letters, always weeks behind, and an occasional one-way, walkie-talkie-type phone call. That first year certainly didn't look like this generation's hyper-documented Instagram grid. Both Dave and Mary knew when he enlisted that this result was a possibility. It didn't make it easier; it was what they needed to do.

When my daughter, Grace, joined the military in 2020, Dave told her before she left for boot camp, "Embrace the suck." He didn't say, "Find the good" or "Pretend it isn't hard" or "Don't make a fool of yourself." Instead, he wanted her to use the uncomfortable as a defining moment of determination, dedication, and self-discovery versus a place to resist or define as bad.

Grace wouldn't be in boot camp forever. She just needed to make it through—learning to run fast, operating on interrupted sleep, and doing things most of us believe we can't survive, all while drill instructors screamed in her face. And she did survive—not because she ran from the hard but because she allowed herself to grow within the hard stuff.

More than that, Grace's beliefs changed in the process. She no longer lived with doubts about her capabilities. Instead, her capabilities and capacity were unearthed in this deeply challenging season. It was hard, for sure. Many times, she had just five minutes to call, and the entire time I'd be saying, "You are strong. You can do this. You need to find that fire within you and not quit."

And she did find that fire. She'll tell you that true strength and purpose is often found in the middle of the uncomfortable. Embracing the suck doesn't mean you agree with the hard or you enjoy it; it means instead of waiting for circumstances to change or for everything to get rosy, you lean in to the uncomfortable and dare to live with joy in the midst. It's not easy, but it allows you to add purpose and intentionality to challenges. It doesn't mean you agree with all the challenges but does allow you not to be a victim within them. It might mean asking yourself, *What can I do today that will bring me joy?* and *What small step can I take now?*

Immediately after boot camp, Grace transitioned to military tech school. She begged me to come visit (there's something awesome about an adult child begging to see you—invest in that time). A couple months and flights later, I stood on a military base and saw my daughter for the first time in months.

She looked the same. Beneath her uniform, her quirky, exuberant personality shone through. But something amazing had happened—the adult in front of me was the *happiest* version of herself I had ever witnessed. This happiness was the result of her hard work, pushing beyond limits, and meeting others with the same drive (including her now-husband, Miguel). If you have children, you might witness it after they study for days for a test and come home with a great grade. And in your own life, it's the happiness found after effort. It's the happiness of pride in oneself and accomplishments.

There was a period of time in my own life, in the years following my divorce, when I didn't feel qualified to feel happy. Happiness felt elusive and selfish, as if I hadn't earned the right to experience that emotion and that only when I fixed things could I *then* be happy. As a result, I found myself dealing with bitterness in the rebuilding years because I wasn't happy and I knew I wanted to be happy. I uncovered, through meditation, journaling, and experience, that happiness starts internally rather than externally. Instead of it being found in things or moments, it is found when you give yourself permission to experience happiness in an imperfect life.

Happiness isn't only reserved for life's perfect moments. Happiness is a beautiful gift found within life's up-and-down timeline. The "I'm not happy" paradigm exists when we wander through life hoping happiness will simply *happen* or looking for it in external places. Yes, there are surprising happy moments, but just like joy, true happiness is something you pursue, embrace, and acknowledge. It's found within life—in doing the hard stuff, dealing with emotions, solving problems, showing up for others, and most important, showing up for yourself and loving your own story.

Right before the end credits roll on an episode of *Survivor*, the contestant who has been voted out shares about their experience. Yes, some are annoyed or frustrated, some are sad, but many of them are genuinely *happy* they were given the opportunity to play.

Your first "get your spark back" step is to ask yourself why you want it back. Then, even if the why is fuzzy, instead of running from challenges, embrace them. Allow yourself to be vulnerable, and with time you will find your happiness again. That happiness may surprise you. It'll be in the simple things, in the moments when you pushed through uncomfortable, the times when you solved issues, as well as the moments of victory when you complete goals you had previously put off.

Whether you're a stay-at-home mom, a professional in the corporate space, in midlife, or an empty nester—whatever your start or story—it's time for you to grab your torch, dip it into the fire, and start.

PS: As much I rave about *Survivor*, I've never submitted my application—until now. When I submitted my final manuscript, I submitted my application as well. I'm ready to take that first step!

## FIRE STARTERS

+ **Do the hard things first.** Instead of putting off doing the uncomfortable, knock the uncomfortable off the list first. Try to not overcommit and overextend. When we overcommit, "I'll do it later" often becomes our response. How can you challenge your "do it later" moments to be "do it now" instead? Expect the uncomfortable to feel uncomfortable, and use the feeling to be a signal that you are doing the hard, brave step.

+ **Look for inspiration.** When I need inspiration, I look to music, movies, and the lives of others. Some of my favorite movies are *The Pursuit of Happyness*, *Rocky*, *Good Will Hunting*, *Erin Brockovich*, *Apollo 13*, and *Rudy*. These movies are motivating because the heroes are ordinary people, like us, who dare to do the extraordinary. I also love YouTube videos of people who overcome obstacles. One of those is of runner Derek Redmond, who suffered a hamstring injury in a semifinal race for the Barcelona Olympics. Despite tremendous pain, he picked himself up and started hobbling toward the finish line. His father, even with security attempting to shoo him away, ran onto the track and held Derek up, helping him across the line. I can't watch it without getting choked up and being inspired to do hard things.[3] Create your own list of movies, books, songs, and true stories that inspire you so you can reach for them when you need a boost.

✦ **Ask "What's the best possible outcome?"** It's so easy to assume the worst. I've found a couple questions that can help immensely with this: "Can I survive that?" and "What's the best possible outcome?" Flipping from a negative to a positive doesn't mean you're denying challenges; instead, you are thinking proactively. This isn't toxic positivity. This is allowing space for real emotions in difficult situations, acknowledging the reality, and then striving to uncover solutions.

# CHAPTER 3

# WHY DO I BELIEVE THIS ABOUT MYSELF?

## *Leaving Self-Imposed Limitations Behind*

Many of our parents were trailblazers. The world we live in now? Our parents created it. My mom challenged gender roles and worked to create equal opportunity for women. If you talked to my mom about this, she'd likely dismiss it. She's feisty yet humble. And because she's humble, I want you to know about a hero in my life, my mom, Linda.

Mom grew up on a farm in southern Minnesota, the fourth youngest of five, and tells tales of chasing chickens, counting pennies, and working hard with her family. Once, while she was standing on dewy grass, my grandfather had her plug something in and she was shocked, but she kept standing—truly the epitome of my mom.

Mom opted to attend college, the first in her family. College in the sixties wasn't like college now, especially business college. Many times, she was the sole woman. Upon seeing that she was the only woman in class, a professor asked her to go get him coffee and to bat her pretty eyelashes while she did it. Can you imagine? Hello, lawsuit. Yet that was the norm for my mom, who dealt with class after class of professors asking her if she was *really* in the right class. She never compromised or backed down. She graduated and moved to Minneapolis, where she married my dad, had us kids, and worked downtown at an international insurance company.

I loved visiting Mom at work. Minneapolis, especially during my childhood, had a vibrant downtown. Not only were there underground tunnels, but every block, between buildings, had skyways connecting them. You could go from building to building and never experience the sub-twenty-degree temps outside. Sometimes Mom would take us to her office and introduce us to coworker after coworker. I don't know if other kids in my class had working moms, but for me it was normal. I also don't truly know the depth of work bias Mom had to punch through, but I can't imagine it was easy.

The older I get, and the more I write about living authentic to your true self, the prouder I am of my mom. She was the OG badass woman, before that term even existed. (Can I call my mom a badass? I just did! Love you, Mom.)

As a kid, I had no idea of how hard my mom worked or the stereotypes she broke.

Once, when I was about ten, after dinner, I was grumbling about how Mom wasn't home. *Again.* It was tax season, when Mom woke early, dropped us off at school, trekked to work, and then worked hours overtime, only to return after we had gone to bed.

My super-hearing dad overheard my disgruntled self and proceeded to push his chair back with dramatic dad flair. Then with exaggerated footsteps he walked in the living room, found my eyes, and sternly told me, "Don't ever complain about how hard your mother works for this family again. Show her respect."

He told me to think about those words while I folded *all* the laundry. Let me just tell you this—when both parents work and your family is exceptionally busy, folding laundry doesn't always make it to the top of the list. Oh, we always had clean laundry, just not *folded* laundry. That night, the Mount Washmore pile of clothes covered the pool table, so I had hours to think about my dad's words.

They stuck.

Mom worked hard, and as a result, I was taught to respect hard work.

Looking back, I can see how much my parents sacrificed to give us the lifestyle I took for granted. Isn't that the way it is? We don't see it in the moment, but as time passes, the picture becomes evident. All the swimming lessons, piano lessons, basketball shoes, volleyball pads, and extracurriculars didn't come from nothing. My parents sacrificed.

In line with their hard-working ethos, a great deal was expected of us kids. Our grades had to be good, and we were to keep up with the above-listed extracurriculars. We were to help at church and speak with respect (part of me suspects my parents kept that laundry pile as a reminder to speak kindly—otherwise, get ready for some folding). We had chores, helped with our massive garden, and maintained the yard. As much as I hated Saturday morning cleaning or shelling peas, it was the expectation, not the exception.

My siblings and I knew the Saturday morning drill and would intentionally watch our cartoons super quietly, hoping our parents wouldn't realize we were awake. And God forbid we fought on a Saturday morning—then we would have the expected chores *and* some extra. Their expectations were high, and thus, we rose to the occasion. In some ways, my childhood was the epitome of "a rising tide lifts all boats."

We rose to meet challenges because that was the expectation placed on each of us. I wasn't ever resentful; instead, this dynamic became the framework in which I learned to operate.

As humans, we rise to the level of expectations around us. My parents expected me to get As and Bs (because they knew I was capable), and because of the expectation, I believed I could achieve those grades. My parents expected me to help in church, and because of their expectations, I hauled chairs around, cleaned up coffee cups, and held babies in the nursery. My parents expected me to find a need and to keep busy without being told, and as a result, with every job I held, I was constantly finding ways to be productive. Their expectations became my reality of self.

Except those times when I realized it was safer to live under the radar.

I experienced bullying as a kid. When you're bullied, you either fight back or hope the bully grows tired. I tried both; both failed. So for the bulk of my school years, I felt the angst of not fitting in. In eighth grade, I scored high enough on the Iowa Test of Basic Skills and was given an opportunity to take the SAT. My parents signed me up and drove me to a community college, where I sat with high schoolers, stared at math problems I didn't understand, and finished the test. The next Monday at school, the principal asked me to share my experience.

No one would talk to me afterward because now I was "too good for" them. My sharing of a triumph led to isolation, and I learned right then: don't be so good at something that people won't want to be your friend. And that led to my under-the-radar limit. I would excel but not so much that others wouldn't like it. I could keep my parents proud and also keep the bullies staved off.

The under-the-radar choice is the ultimate in defense. No one could say I wasn't trying. I was still getting good grades, still participating, still doing what needed to be done. I would go so far . . . and then I'd back off, back into the undetectable zone. I didn't realize this was my strategy until years later.

The limit I had created? Be good enough but not too good.

Good enough but not too good only works so long without creating frustration. It didn't get me out of my first marriage; it only kept me staying in dysfunction. It doesn't create change; it creates stagnation and agitation. Good enough but not too good leaves your soul gasping for air. Good enough requires work to maintain the status quo, but it doesn't propel you forward.

I wanted to be great, to live without the shallow breaths of good enough.

## DON'T PLAY IT SAFE

In the summer of 2020, I started seeing a counselor again. I was smack in the middle of those years of getting out of my way, and I found myself very much *in my way*. Being in the middle of the pandemic didn't help, although it did allow me to have a starting point to talk about. The first time I sat in her office, after the niceties, she asked me to explain what I was looking for. "I'm tired of feeling like I'm under the radar, but I can't figure out what to do to change it." I knew I was playing smaller than I could be.

I had broken out of so many things: a bad marriage, terrible finances, and yet, underneath all of that, part of me was still whispering, *Play it safe, Rachel. Don't make a scene.* Friends and coworkers could see my potential, but when it came time to make the big leap, instead of jumping, I'd balk.

Even though I disliked this part of myself, I couldn't seem to stop the cycle. Have you experienced this? You know you need to change something, but you have no idea how? It is ridiculously frustrating. How could I be trying to ignite my spark and at the same time be putting it out? It's like trying to light wet wood—it just won't happen. The issue wasn't that I didn't want to change or that I wasn't trying—the issue was that I was attempting to light wet wood.

You can't start a fire without the proper fuel. Until I recognized that the issue was my patterns, beliefs, and limitations, that fire wasn't going to burn. You can spend time, energy, and money trying to figure yourself out, but until you remove the wet wood (old patterns) and add healthy fuel to the fire, those old patterns will compete with who you strive to be.

I didn't meet with that counselor thinking I was the limitation. I went to figure out what action steps I needed to *do*, not to change internally. I had frustrated those around me with my worrying, my waiting, and my self-doubt, which only added to my frustration. I kept trying to light the wet wood, to no avail. No one could understand why I couldn't get it to light. They could see how far I had come, how much I had overcome, and didn't understand why I couldn't take the next step. What they didn't see was that it wasn't about lighting the old but rather confronting why I kept trying to relight a pattern that wasn't working.

My counselor and I didn't work on my under-the-radar fear for a while. Instead, I shared about my childhood and the bullying, my parents and their expectations, my first marriage and the emotional and financial havoc, my years as a single mother, the self-doubt, and about my new marriage and blended family adaptations. I shared with her this fear of speaking up, as if speaking up would result in me getting blackballed. Instead of judging or giving answers, she'd ask, "Why do you believe that to be true?"

Often, I had evidence—evidence of the bullying or of business deals gone sour when I spoke up and fought for myself. Other times, it was just me assuming I'd get hurt, assuming others would respond in a negative way. Finally, about a year into our sessions, I looked up at her with realization and said, "I'm the one keeping myself under the radar."

I'd spent years blaming everyone and everything else, but at the core, no one but me was holding me back. I think she knew this the whole time but needed me to go through the unraveling and realization myself. For so long, I believed the "wood" was dry, and until I could see it wasn't, no matter how much I pushed myself to change, my soul's fire was incapable of igniting.

Instead of more effort, I needed to remove the limitation.

No one likes to think about self-imposed limitations. It was more comfortable to put the responsibility on the past and not my own beliefs. When you step out from under the radar, you risk being seen. A teacher in our school district shared on Facebook a nomination she had received for Teacher of the Year. She publicly asked parents to go to the website, find her picture, and to vote for her. This meant she was willing to accept no votes as well as yes votes. She was willing to have other teachers think, *Who does she think she is?* She fought for it. That is vulnerable. But I can guarantee stepping out into the light gave her many more votes than those who thought, *I can't put myself out there like that; what will others think?* or *What if no one votes for me?*

You won't get votes if you don't ask for votes.

You might have limitations imposed on your story. Some could stem from your upbringing, from failures, from bullying, from circumstances out of your control, or from times when success brought out the critics. Some limitations have root causes out of our control, while other limitations were most likely created to keep you safe. Is it possible that those limits are too restrictive? Is it possible that those limits prevent you from stepping out of your comfort zone? The antidote to a playing-it-safe, under-the-radar mindset is to challenge what the mindset is protecting you from. There's a good chance you'll have an idea. Most of the time, we place these limitations on ourselves to avoid embarrassment or others talking about us or possible failure.

While these limitations might protect you from potential negative outcomes, they also hinder potential amazing outcomes.

Don't accept a story too small for your greatness.

## MOVING PAST "IF ONLY"

My husband, Dan, has a history of competitive running. He's an excellent athlete but is humble about his feats, so I'm going to brag a bit. Dan has completed an Ironman and a ridiculous number of triathlons as well as running or swimming in numerous other races. His running story inspired my running story. Whenever I have a running question, I go to him first because he has put in the time and effort to have answers I trust.

Like all of us, Dan has a moment of *if only* as part of his story. You know those stories—"If only I had tried . . ." "If only I had spoken up . . ." "If only I didn't quit . . ." "If only I hadn't forgotten . . ." Dan's *if only* moment happened while running on his high school's cross-country team. They had some fast runners, kids who were part of running clubs outside of school as well. These kids typically won every race, which is where Dan's *if only* moment starts.

I loved being on the cross-country team. I wasn't fast like Mike and Dave, the top guys on our team. In cross-country, the top five runners of each team score points, so it was my goal to at least be number five.

In my *if only* race, the starting gun went off, and we all took off across a field. Eight or nine schools were competing, so we were strewn wide across the field. And when the gun went off, we all ran toward an opening in the trees on the other side.

It was a bit of a mad scramble, but I made it unscathed and navigated the curves and hills until we reached the one-mile point. It was marked by a giant "one" sign next to the trail. And the coaches were there yelling out times.

That's when I noticed Mike and Dave running next to me. We were in front, maybe not first place but in the top ten for sure. Seeing them was jarring; it took me off my game.

I immediately felt like I had made a mistake, like I didn't belong there and should get back to where I belong before I ran out of energy and died from starting too fast. I slowed down to the pace I thought I was supposed to be at.

I physically slowed down because my brain told me I didn't belong there.

If only I could have that moment back. Of all the moments in my life I'd like to get back, I'd pick that moment. Even now, at fifty years old, it makes me teary thinking about it. Why didn't I just try to keep going? What if I *didn't* run out of energy? What if for once in my life I actually won? I can't imagine how much confidence I would have taken into the rest of high school. What if I had overcome that moment of fear and tried—and was able to finish with Mike and Dave for the rest of the races that season? What if instead of always feeling like the chubby kid who just wanted to be part of the team, I actually *was* part of the team?

I can't believe this memory is making me teary. I just wish I had that moment back. Please . . . can I have that one moment back?

Unlike me, Dan wasn't afraid of being seen but rather believed he wasn't capable of being faster. In my life, I knew I could go farther, but I kept myself smaller. But Dan believed that he couldn't move beyond the radar's line. Instead of challenging the limitation that he wasn't the best runner and couldn't win, he accepted the cap as the truth of his potential. What if the only difference between him and Mike and Dave was that they believed they could win? Is it possible believing he could be the winner might have changed the outcome?

On the surface, Dan's "limit" might not even be challenged. He knew his race pace and was comfortable with it. That day, he decided that his initial speed wasn't maintainable because it was faster than his customary pace. Even though this race was weeks into the season, Dan still believed he could only run his standard race pace instead of expecting to get faster as the season progressed.

Sometimes we don't know we have placed a limit on ourselves. Dan was excited about being fifth on the team and was content with his perceived spot. But that contentment also put a limit on his speed. Instead of pushing to get faster, he kept a regulator on his potential. Then, when the limit was exposed, instead of pushing through, he held back because it was where he believed he needed to exist.

What he *believed* he could do was less than he actually could do. Dan would have fought to stay in fifth but didn't believe he could be fourth. In our own lives, these limits are harder to identify because they are often steeped within our identity. Dan's identity was being the fifth-place finisher, and because he accepted it as truth, instead of busting through the limit when it was challenged, he settled back to what he knew.

Your life might have limits that cause you to settle into a truth smaller than your potential. Is your limit high enough? Or could you go higher? Why do you have the limit in the first place? Sometimes the limit is linked to our education or training. Maybe you think you'll only go so far in your career because you don't have a degree. With this belief, you may convince yourself not to email a dream company you'd like to work for and put yourself out there, never opening the door to what could be the greatest job in the world.

Maybe you believe you can only be so good at guitar because you've never had formal lessons. When your friends ask you to play with them at church, you decline because you believe you can't play with those who have different training. But what if you *are* good enough and can keep up with the rest of the band? Your self-imposed limit is keeping you from potentially making new friends and having a creative outlet.

After high school, when Dan's environment changed, his expectations of himself changed too. He broke through that prior self-imposed limit. He kept running, kept competing, and went on to finish dozens of triathlons and an Ironman. You don't just sign up to complete an Ironman on a whim—you sign up because you believe you *can* swim 2.4 miles, bike 112 miles, and run a full marathon within sixteen to seventeen hours.

His expectation of self changed from, "I can only do this much" to "What could I do?"

## RAISE THE BAR

In track and field, coaches sometimes raise the bar for their high jumpers without them knowing, just to push the jumper to a level they didn't think was possible. If you want to raise the bar in your own life, you need to examine the limits you've put in place to keep you safe or those you think are unbreakable. Raising the bar is expecting more of yourself, which will mean pushing back on your own thinking.

What could your life look like if you raise your own bar? Let's look at four areas where we might be keeping our bar too low.

## 1. The Past

As a child, I had a real fear of being bullied, and that trickled into my adult life. The unspoken bar was: Why be a standout if it means you might be laughed at? I had to become okay with possibly being laughed at. I had to become okay with others not liking me. I had to become okay with not being a part of the in-crowd. The low bar I had set assumed others, not bullies, would choose the same response to success as the ones in the past did.

Can you identify some areas in your past that caused you to limit your expectations of yourself? Areas where you've steered toward self-protection at the expense of taking risks or achieving? Responses from the past can keep your bar set lower than it should be—and that bar follows many of us into adulthood.

Choose to set your bar in the present, not based off the past. This means challenging your bar (like Dan did) instead of simply accepting it as the limit. For example, if you were told in seventh grade that you were a terrible singer and you've allowed that to be your truth in your forties, that limit is based on the past. What if you're the greatest singer in the world and the past words were meant to keep you small? Do you want to live your entire life based on the "truth" from your thirteen-year-old self?

Asking, "Why do I believe this to be true?" is the best antidote to beliefs rooted in the past.

Another way to bust through these limits is to start trying things again. Join the YMCA's basketball team, the choir, the neighborhood book club, or the morning walking group. When you create action, you will naturally begin to challenge limits on your time and potential. You will also open doors to trying new things—maybe you'll see another class at the Y, will play piano, will organize another book club, or will start to run in the mornings. Every bit of limit-busting action creates momentum.

## 2. The Way It's Always Been

There are some bars in life that are untested. These are the things we grew up doing, we were taught, or it's just the way it's always been. The best example of this is an old wives' tale I once heard. It goes like this: One day, this gal got ready to bake a ham for her family. She pulled out the cutting board, got a knife, and proceeded to cut the ends off the ham. As the ham baked and the aroma filled her home, she began to wonder why she cut the ends off. Was it a secret? Who better to ask than her mom? She called her mom up, curious about the response. Well, then, her mom, who also cuts the ends off the ham before baking, told her daughter she, too, didn't know. So together, they called the girl's grandmother, curious about this family secret. Grandma answered, heard the question, and burst out laughing.

"I cut the ends off because otherwise it didn't fit in my baking pan."

For years, in that tale, everyone accepted that the "normal" way to make ham was to cut off the ends. Uncovering these limits requires you to question those going-through-the-motion responses in your life. Some limits might be impractical or no longer needed.

If you find yourself doing something because that's the way you always do it, today's the day to challenge that bar. There might be a better way home, a tastier au gratin potato recipe, a new side of the church to sit in. Don't operate an autopilot; start asking the questions.

### 3. The Environment

I took the ACT twice. Because I went to an incredibly small high school (I graduated with fifteen other seniors), testing location options were limited. The first testing location was a dark, musty library at a round table with two other people. The proctor was cranky, and the lighting was terrible. And any sense of autonomy or privacy was lost because of how close we were sitting. I told my mom after how awful the space was and that I knew I didn't do my best.

I was unhappy with the first score, so I decided to take it again—at a different location too. I chose a fancy prep school on the other side of town. This time, I sat at a desk in a light-filled classroom. My score went up six points. Sure, I had more time to learn before that second test. But I also knew that the environment had made an enormous difference for me.

Your surroundings have the potential to affect your outlook—whether it's the physical space or the people you've surrounded yourself with. Maybe you were told that "people like you" can accomplish only certain things. Perhaps no one in your family has done what you dream of doing (like my mom being the first woman in her family to go to college). Maybe you were told not to dream so big. Maybe you've carried an unchallenged limitation (like Dan) into your current surroundings. Pay attention to your surroundings. Pay attention to the words others use to describe you and the words you use to describe yourself.

Sometimes addressing your environment means cutting ties so you can raise your bar. If you want to quit drinking but all your current friends like to get sloshed on Friday nights, you must step out of an environment that doesn't promote your growth. Losing friends is never easy, but if they don't support your dreams and goals, it might be a critical step. And in time, when those friends see the new you, with a different bar set for yourself, they may want some of that goodness for themselves.

## 4. The Limits of Practicality

Actor and comedian Jim Carrey, in his 2014 commencement speech to Maharishi International University, charged each student with the responsibility to live a life of integrity, passion, and purpose. Partway into the speech, he recounted how his father, also a comedian, took a safe job—and then ended up losing it, which left the family scraping. Then Carrey famously said, "You can fail at what you don't want, so you might as well take a chance on doing what you love."[4]

Carrey called out the limit of practicality cloaked in playing it safe. Unlike his father, Jim Carrey chose the unpractical route. He became the dreamer, the doer, and the risk-taker. He saw the results of dreams dashed and knew that his time on the earth would be daring.

I know so many who have lived beneath the limit of practicality. They know they have potential, but fear of the unknown—finances, potential whispers of "Who does she think she is?," breaking out of what is expected—keeps them exactly where they are, with dreams just above their own self-imposed and safe bar. We all have these self-imposed bars too. These might be the bars of religion, education, family, or expectations. To move the limit, you need to identify the limit. The best way to do that? Ask yourself, just like my counselor challenged me, *Why do I believe this to be true?*

You are worthy and capable of limits beyond what you and others have set as possible. Your true self, your vibrant, quirky, boisterous, dreamer self is enough to excel. And *you* get to move that bar to a place that feels right for you. Some of these bars might be easy to see or reframe, and others will take soul searching. We sometimes must confront a lifetime of unspoken "truths" that we have adopted as infallible. The first step is asking yourself, *Why do I believe I cannot break this?* followed by, *Does keeping this bar hinder me or help me?* The third step is asking, *Could I break through this limit?*

Your old story's limits don't get to define your present potential.

## TO NEW HEIGHTS

The number-one way I've found to discover limits is to put myself out there, to try new things, and to say yes (instead of defaulting to "I'll do that later" or "It's not the right time"). For the past decade, on January 1, I've chosen a word for the upcoming year. My words have ranged from *brave* to *resolute* to *happy*. When 2024 rolled around, I immediately knew my word was *confident*. I wanted to live confident enough to be seen *above* the radar, to try new things, to raise my bar, and to let go of anything holding me back. Perhaps what I'm doing will help you raise your bar and hit new heights.

## Practice Mindfulness Daily

I typically meditate in the morning. Some mornings, it's for just two minutes, some for twenty. I allow my mind to be still, and in the stillness, I ask myself, *What can I do to make today great?* Whether you meditate, pray, walk, or have other practices that support your spirit, there is great power in being still and letting yourself reflect. This pause moment allows you to respond versus react. A response gives you control, while a reaction happens immediately. Mindfulness not only allows the brain to rest, but it also clears your mind of externals, which then allows you to connect with your deeper self.

Mindfulness creates space that allows you to move from "Why am I doing this?" to "What will I do next?"

It opens pathways for deliberate, thoughtful responses rather than living in a state of reactivity.

## Challenge Yourself

I try every month to put myself in new situations that are visible and uncomfortable. These are some of the out-of-the-box experiences from my last six months.

On New Year's Day in 2024, I jumped in a freezing lake. I climbed into a cryofreeze chamber at −156 degrees with my amazing friend Catherine. I ran a 5K in pouring rain on my birthday (last year I probably would have canceled). I tried acroyoga with a colleague I had met hours prior in a tiny, landscaped area (this is two-person yoga where one person balances on the other).

Before I dunked my head in that frigid lake on January 1, I asked myself, *Why are you so afraid of doing this?* The answer? I didn't want to be cold and uncomfortable. At first it was, *I hate cold water.* Then I asked myself, *Can you* survive *cold water?* I knew I could. On the drive there, I kept telling myself on repeat, *You are stronger than cold. You are stronger than cold. You are stronger than cold.*

The wind was whipping that day, making it even colder. *You are stronger than cold.*

Millie, Dan's then-fourteen-year-old-daughter, had already dunked her head under. My legs were shaking. Why were we doing this ridiculous thing?

*You are stronger than cold.*

I took a breath. And I went under.

It was ridiculously cold. When I stood up, because I was so cold, I fell back in.

*You are stronger than cold.*

This may seem like a little thing, but it was a huge mental achievement for me! I survived. I made it. I'm not cold today. What finally pushed me to go under was one question: "What will you regret more?" For me, that would have been getting all the way there, putting my feet in, and deciding I couldn't do it. Wimping out.

I've also said yes to things that needed to be done but that I've been avoiding. I've known for several years (okay, twenty years) that I needed to have dental work done to replace two molars I wasn't born with. I've avoided this—partly due to the cost, partly due to putting everyone else first, and partly due to the potential pain. But, living with the word *confident*, I knew it was time. So as I'm finishing these edits, I'm also nursing a tender jaw from going through the surgery days ago.

Challenge yourself to do not only the new and the fun things but also all those things you've been putting off.

Would you agree to put it off if it was your kids? Or your spouse? Or your best friend? If the answer is no, take that as a sign to make it a yes for yourself. Every single yes will fill your heart, your flame, with more confidence, and you will find yourself more confident. Every single yes will grow your confidence.

### Record Your Wins, Good Days, and Limit-Busting Moments

Today we're going to change your calendar. From now on, I want you to begin to document the great moments in life. Post a Facebook update with pictures from a trip; add "Today Was an Awesome Day" to your Google alerts; get out the red Sharpie and circle the Thursday when you felt on top of the world. Here's why: it can be easy to remember the hard days and challenges and forget how unstoppable and awesome you are as well.

Have you ever taken first- and last-day-of-school pictures? I make my kids take them each year (even the high schoolers). Where I take them never changes—it's next to the front door—and as a result, there is a visible representation of their changes in height and appearance. I don't notice the change as it's happening, but that one picture powerfully illustrates their growth. As you change in life, you might not even notice or remember it happening.

Recording wins, taking pictures, and creating a record of victories will inspire you when the inevitable bad day happens or when you think, *Does any of this even matter?*

Start writing down all the amazing steps you've taken. Document your walks, your runs, the times when you show up for cooking class or a trip to the dentist. Start to record these victories and breakthroughs. This list will inspire you to keep going, to keep adding, and hopefully, in the end will remind you that you, just like my mom, are a badass.

Something else happens when you raise your bar: you get stuff done. I no longer have "get dental implants" on my list of items rolling over from year to year. The more you accomplish, the more you will believe you can accomplish. And finally, you will gain the confidence that next time you need to do something hard, you will survive.

You are worthy of raising the bar in your life and pushing beyond the radar's limitations.

## FIRE STARTERS

+ **Define your expectations.** I have expectations for my kids—be kind, complete your assignments, speak respectfully to your teachers, be involved in an extracurricular. I'm guessing you do as well. But what are your expectations for your *life?* If you don't know, ask yourself something like, *What six life lessons do I want my kids to know?* Think through the answers and why those lessons mean something to you—and then apply them to your own life. When you take the time to define your expectations of self, you also challenge the expectations that no longer serve you.

✦ **Examine your self-imposed limits.** Ask yourself what it would take to prove that your self-limitations are real. For instance, if you don't believe you can run a 5K but I bet you a thousand dollars you can, would you sign up, train, and finish? Or would you do all that work and not finish? At some point, limits become possibilities. My kids will often tell me something is too hard, but then if I hypothetically offer them a reward, they immediately recognize that the supposed difficulty isn't holding them back; they just don't want to take the time or endure the discomfort of completing the task. Reframe what you think you can't do as if an incentive is involved, and see if your limits change.

# CHAPTER 4

# HOW DO I FIND MY SPARK?

## Looking Back to Look Forward

Have you watched the Michael J. Fox documentary, *Still?* I can't recommend it enough. It chronicles Fox's career from child actor in *Family Ties* to megastar in *Back to the Future* to his Parkinson's diagnosis to now. It's hard to reconcile the guitar-strumming Marty McFly with his body now and the debilitating neurological effects Parkinson's has had on him. The title is clever, poetic, and poignant—while the disease has taken his ability to remain still, he is still here, stronger than ever. In the years since his diagnosis, Fox has raised more than $2 billion for Parkinson's research. He may not be speeding to eighty-eight miles per hour in a DeLorean, but he is changing the future for millions.

The opening scene is a reenactment of the moment when Fox first suspected something wasn't right. His pinky finger was trembling on its own. For a split second, he hoped it was a moth landing on his finger, flapping its wings, but deep down he knew his finger was shaking on its own.

Fox calls that moment "a message from the future."[5] That twitching finger was the first clue of what was to come. He didn't know it then, but his present self could look back and see there was a sign. Many times, we don't look backward in our quest for self-discovery. While the past doesn't need to define tomorrow, there are some moments in our past that foreshadow who and what is to come.

Not all messages from the future are beacons of coming challenges like Fox's was. Many are markers waiting to be found again. Growing up, my family spent our Saturdays fishing on Lake Minnetonka, about twenty miles west of Minneapolis. My dad's parents owned a boat, named the *Crusader*, and docked her about a mile from their home. After digging up worms in the garden, we'd trek down to my grandparents' home, where we'd say hello (and I'd convince Grandma I needed some cookies), and then we'd go to the dock, get in the boat, and navigate through bays and lake channels to our fishing spot.

Sometimes when the fishing was "hot," we'd leave a marker—a giant floating bobber (often a milk jug) with an anchor. The marker would hopefully stay in the same spot, reminding us where to return. Sometimes we'd see other people's markers and would pull up next to them, drop in our lines, and hope the fish would bite.

Messages from the future are like markers in your story's timeline. Some are super visible, and some are tucked underneath events and memories. But they are there, like that bobber, waiting to be found.

## PAYING ATTENTION TO THE MESSAGES

I know some of you love this idea of finding your spark and yet don't have a clue *who* you are, *what* you want to do, or where that bobber is in life. If that's you, breathe. You're not alone, and we will figure it out, but it will take being willing to trust yourself (and me) as you examine some of your own message markers from the future.

It starts with being willing to look back and to talk with others about your life. When I started to wonder what I could do that would make me happy, I discovered two marker events from my past that were foreshadowing my future.

First, I liked public speaking. Twenty years ago, after my son Brennan was born, I attended a Tuesday-morning women's group led by a vivacious and unconventional woman named Patti. Looking back, I credit Patti for encouraging me to wonder about the boxes I'd confined myself to and for challenging me to break out. Although it was nine years before results could be seen, my courage in attending those Tuesday mornings was the start of profound internal change—from unearthing limits, to no longer accepting them, to the action to change them.

The beginnings of change are rarely visible to outsiders. Most successful people will tell you about the unseen years of hustle before they were "discovered." Typically, we don't witness the hustle, the before—we just see the after. The after is often loud, visible, and life-changing, and those invisible years prior are often dismissed or diluted. The same is true for the hard moments in life. Rarely is a major challenge a one-time event but rather a series of events percolating until the outside world sees the outcome of what you've been enduring.

After several months, Patti asked if I'd be interested in sharing my breaking-out-of-the-box realizations with the group (about a hundred women). Despite my lack of public speaking experience, I was intrigued, so I said yes. The next week, I found myself behind a podium sharing about the ugly, uncomfortable, and yet redeeming places in my life. *I wonder if anyone can see my hands shaking*, I thought. Despite the external shake, my heart had unexpectedly found its place.

I loved sharing, loved storytelling, but most of all loved offering nuggets of hope. I lifted my bar's limit and shared about how I was tired of letting life happen to me and that I was determined to change. I was vulnerable and real and could see women nodding, handing each other tissues, and saying, "Amen." In that moment, I remember thinking, *I could do this; this is what I'm called to do*.

Eight years later, I was the opening keynote for a homeschooling conference in Pennsylvania and since then have keynoted dozens of events worldwide. That glimmer of interest in speaking turned into a career.

The second marker moment involved my childhood summers. Our family typically took a road trip, our gray conversion van towing a pop-up camper and my folks navigating with maps and AAA TripTiks. My dad, the engineer, loves data. He recorded our miles traveled, stops, and average miles per gallon in a notebook kept between the seats. One year, on a trip to Utah, my job was to record the data.

I had forgotten about my data duties until one day almost thirty years in the future, when my writing career was in its infancy. Writing is what ultimately changed my story. It unlocked the doors to financial change and created opportunities to share my heart with the world. But in the beginning, when I was still uncertain about my capabilities, my dad told me, "I always knew you could be a writer."

He called me a writer—years before I felt comfortable calling myself a writer.

Curious, I asked him how he knew. And then he shared a message from the future in the form of those mileage notebooks from years ago, notebooks he wished he'd kept. Although my job was to record info, Dad told me I would write about the places and people we were seeing and create a narrative from the ordinary.

My dad's recollection boosted my confidence. In 2008, I started my blog. In 2013, I published my first eBook. In 2018, I published my first physical book. In 2023, I published my second book. And this book was written because I confidently can now say that I am not only a writer but also an author.

Even if you can't see them now, your life has messages from the future bobbing on the surface of your past. These messages are beacons of light, sparks of possibility about things you love, are great at, could do, and enjoy. They might offer a solution in your life like they did for me. My career is built on speaking and writing, and now, looking back, not only can I see those two messages but dozens more.

*One fall day, my then-sixteen-year-old son, Elijah, came out of his room, bypassed the kitchen (rare indeed), and handed me twenty dollars. Before I could ask what it was for, he said, "Could you buy something for me on my computer that costs eighteen dollars?"*

*I said sure, but like every mom of a teenager, I asked him what it was for. He said, "I am buying a server." Thankfully, I know a bit about coding and computers, so I pressed for info and asked what kind of server. He then told me how he and his friends had built a game for the site Steam and needed a server to host it on.*

*"You're doing what?" I was so impressed, especially because I grew up coding. All the time he was in his room, sitting on his computer, talking loudly with his friends, he was creating something. I had assumed he was just playing, but in the midst of playing he discovered something he was good at. Sometimes I wonder if that, coupled with his acing of every single science and math class, will be a message to his future self.*

Your responsibility is to find your messages. They are there, just waiting for you to unearth them. Now, sometimes fear will tell you the discovered marker message is too big, too hard, too challenging, or too late for you to breathe life into it again. Instead of sinking into the fear, I want you to examine that fear. Fear isn't always a red light telling you to stop. Sometimes fear is an indicator that you are on the right track. Remember, anticipation often feels like fear.

I encourage you to greet your fear as a friend who is there to help you determine your path forward. Instead of seeing fear as a red light, ask yourself why you feel the fear. Maybe you're scared simply because you don't know the steps to move past it, not because it's a legitimate fear telling you not to move forward. Can you allow yourself time to go on this journey? Every time you question fear, it is like lighting a candle in a dark room. At first you can only sort of see, but as your eyes adjust, the light begins to overtake the darkness.

Start examining your life. At the end of this chapter, in the Fire Starters section, I've included a list of fifty questions to help you start to uncover your own message markers. Explore them. Meditate on them. Start to wonder about you again. And if fear starts creeping in, remember to link arms with it as your friend and ask it to reveal deeper truths.

One of my favorite quotes, often attributed to Eleanor Roosevelt, is, "Do one thing every day that scares you." I've chosen to live these words. And you can too! Looking for your message markers might unearth some fears. But what if on the other side of fear is happiness? For years, especially before challenging days, I've told my kids Roosevelt's quote. Then, one day, after reminding me of Roosevelt's words, my son Elijah remarked, "Mom, you have another sign in the kitchen that says, 'Do one thing every day that makes you happy.'"

That was the day when fear no longer was something to be feared. That day I realized that oftentimes on the other side of fear is happiness.

## DECISION PARALYSIS

If you were to ask my husband where he grew up, he'd respond with, "Which year?" His dad remained in the Air Force throughout Dan's childhood, and as a result, he grew up as a military brat, moving from base to base across the country. Dan has never told me his favorite base, but if I had to guess, based on the number of tales, it probably would be Elmendorf Air Force Base in Anchorage, Alaska. There, his elementary school years consisted of not only math, spelling, and science but also regular sonic booms from the F-15 military jets training overhead.

His early life consisted of moving boxes, meeting new people, and establishing roots, only to move again and start over. My life was the opposite. In 1977, my parents built the suburban Minneapolis split-level home they still reside in. Their home is a catalog of life moments and memories—some still etched into pavers or inked onto walls. While they never moved, we did take epic family vacations. Dan saw the world in moving, and I saw it in road trip miles logged across North America. Even though our childhoods varied, the spark of travel exists within both of us, and we've passed it on to our blended family. Several times a year, we'll pack up the kids, load up the vehicles, and take a trek. We've journeyed to both Minnesota and the Gulf of Mexico multiple times; to the Ozarks; Washington, DC; Philadelphia; Savannah; the Outer Banks; and pretty much every Tennessee state park.

Hanging in our office is a gigantic United States map with roads we've traveled highlighted in red. Instead of just coloring in visited states, we shade in the roads. Then, when the "Where are we going this year?" question hits in early spring, the first step is to reference the map of where we've already been. I love the ocean—it's a sacred space of peace for me—and will seek it out, which resulted in spring break 2023 being spent in Navarre Beach, Florida. Navarre Beach is on the Gulf Coast, between Destin and Pensacola on a section of shore called the Emerald Coast. It's an exquisite, picture-perfect gem tucked in Florida's Panhandle.

It's also the destination that almost wasn't, due to decision paralysis.

Decision paralysis is an inability to make a decision due to the fear of making the wrong decision. I've struggled with decision-making most of my life. I would fret over decisions, worry if a choice was correct, and oftentimes, as soon as I'd decide, I'd immediately doubt myself instead of proceeding forward. It's hard to make progress if you're living in a loop of decision paralysis.

For that trip, I took on the responsibility of finding the rental home for our large family. My task? Find a place within budget that still boasted ocean views and was close enough to cool places the teenagers could walk to. Since VRBO and Airbnb don't give an exact address until you book, I would go to Google maps, try to find the rental, and then scope out the surrounding area. I'd scour reviews and look for real estate listings. This was all my own doing. Dan just wanted a clean place, somewhere to put his head, and a home base for us to sleep, shower, and get some breakfast. His goal was not to be in the rental but to be out in the world exploring.

After a couple days of searching (yes, days), I sent a potential rental to Dan to check out. It was across the street from the beach, had beachy décor and enough beds (this is critical), and was within budget. He looked at my link, liked the price, and immediately booked it.

I instantly felt regret.

> *What if it's the wrong place?*
> *What if it isn't big enough?*
> *What if it's noisy?*
> *What if the reviews aren't right?*
> *What if it's too far for the kids to walk to the boardwalk?*
> *What if, what if, what if?*

Our brains can be *loud*, especially when the decision loop begins. This time, instead of mulling the doubts internally, I worry-vomited my concerns on Dan. At first, he was chill, but as my questions kept coming, his level of tolerance lowered. After a bit, he said that despite potentially losing over $1,000 in a nonrefundable deposit, he was going to find a new place to alleviate my whirlwind of worry and to allow his peace to return. When I realized what my worry was causing, I stopped in my tracks.

I've come up with four reasons for decision paralysis as well as four solutions to either prevent it or halt it when you are in the middle of it.

## DECISION PARALYSIS REASON 1: FEAR OF MAKING THE WRONG DECISION

No one likes to make the wrong decision. And we don't intend to make the wrong decision either. No one goes into the decision-making process thinking, *I'm going to choose the worst possible outcome for myself and my family.* You make decisions with the knowledge you have in front of you and the lessons you've learned behind you. Times when you made a decision that didn't work out can cause you to overquestion yourself. It's not that you can't decide; you just don't want to risk the outcome of the wrong decision.

### Solution: Ask Yourself, "Can I Survive a Bad Decision?"

If your answer to this question is no, that's your first clue to reevaluate. Most decisions can be adapted and are survivable. Let's say my family had arrived at our rental and it was a hellhole, bedbug-infested dump. We wouldn't have stayed there, we would have adapted, and we would have had a story to tell for years to come!

I realized my fear over making a "wrong" decision was deeper than just booking the wrong place. It was rooted in two things: fear of making a bad financial decision and fear of letting my family down. Because of my financial past, the idea of spending money on something horrible froze me. Second, because these trips are a huge deal in our family, I didn't want anyone to hate the place we were staying and potentially ruin the trip. I could have lost us money, and the place could have been horrible. But neither of those things happened. The paralysis happened in the hypothetical pondering of potential negatives.

As you begin to decide how you're going to spend your time investing in finding your spark, be prepared, especially in the beginning, for the negatives to speak louder than the positives. If I had listened to the negatives, our beach trip would have been a "what might have been"; instead, it was a wonderful memory.

Oddly, sometimes the bad decisions create the best memories. Once, when Dan was young, his family stayed at a not-so-great motel on the way to Spokane, Washington. The motel was nasty—dirty, cups-in-the-sink gross. Dan's little brother, Tom, who was three at the time, announced, "This place is the *first worst*." The term *first worst* has stuck in Dan's family ever since, all because of a theoretically poor choice more than forty years ago. And now? Now it makes everyone laugh.

## DECISION PARALYSIS REASON 2: AVOIDANCE

I bought into a belief that I'm a poor decision-maker. As a result, I'd either avoid making a decision or overly question decisions. Avoidance is a form of procrastination. Avoidance finds other things to do or tells us decisions can't be made without all the information. The problem with waiting for information is that you'll never get it all or the information will change. Avoidance says, "Just wait"—without a timeline.

Avoidance gives away your power to others and circumstances. You might think you're waiting on a decision, but you are actually making a decision to *give away* your decision. Avoidance is also a desert: eventually, you'll be so thirsty that you'll do anything for water, and if it's regarding decision-making, you'll make any decision out of desperation.

### Solution: Add a Deadline, and Learn to Trust Yourself

Don't wait until you're parched, and don't give away your decision-making right.

True confidence results in reclaiming decision-making control and accepting the results of the decision. It means being okay with great, mediocre, fabulous, and terrible results. It also means being okay with accepting a new identity as the confident decision-maker as opposed to the person who needs to run every option by everyone else. This is the start of learning to trust yourself. Trusting yourself doesn't mean you're arrogant or that you don't hear the opinions of others. It's the opposite. Trusting yourself puts the responsibility of decisions back on you and removes the potential for you to default to, "Well, I shouldn't have listened to them." Confidence replaces blame with ownership.

But how, right? Avoidance's biggest lie is this: you have unlimited time. News flash: you don't. However, you *will* fill your time one way or the other—whether you make a decision to try to find your spark, to change your narrative, to forgive, to seek happiness, and to take care of yourself, or you don't. You might fill that time with worry, Netflix, or frustration. The absence of a tough decision means you're defaulting to a passive, seemingly easier, yet temporary decision.

Making decisions is a powerful catalyst. The more confident you become in making decisions, the easier it will be to stand up for yourself. Your ability to discern what is important will improve, and the need to defend or doubt your decisions will lessen. What if you're one decision away from stepping onto the path you've told yourself you can't find? The only way you'll know is to actually decide and stick with your decision.

## DECISION PARALYSIS REASON 3: YOU FEEL LIKE YOU DON'T KNOW YOURSELF

If you're stalling out on figuring out what you like because you don't know who you are, you've successfully created a catch-22. You can't figure out what you like until you know who you are, and you can't figure out who you are until you know what you like.

Which comes first, the chicken or the egg? Figuring out what you like or who you are?

### Solution: Ask Yourself, "What If the Ordinary Is the Extraordinary?"

If each of us intrinsically knew our calling, life would be pretty boring. There wouldn't be the need to innovate, to explore, and to create. And what if there wasn't just one perfect calling either? What if you gave yourself the grace to learn a new skill or pursue a new passion?

For most of us, there isn't a moment in life when we will be like, "This is it! I've figured everything out! I know who I am!" You aren't meant to stay stagnant; you are on a journey of continuous discovery within the ordinary. Yes, the ordinary.

Let's face it: most of life is ordinary. Most of our days don't consist of the grand trips or milestone moments. Rather, daily life is often the same thing, coupled with time passing by. And I truly believe that finding your spark happens within the ordinary.

It starts with being willing to appreciate the in-between, the normal—sunrises, hot lattes with friends, laughter, taking a walk. Learn to love that you get to wake in the morning and do something with your day. You get the opportunity to reignite your life. And in doing something, you are writing the next chapter of your story.

"Who am I?" changes with time, with age, and with experience. Give yourself grace to live within the unknown of the ordinary, to let who you are change with time, and to let your ordinary become your extraordinary story.

## DECISION PARALYSIS REASON 4: I NEED TO KNOW I'M 100 PERCENT MAKING THE RIGHT DECISION

Even if every single variable is locked down and you feel 120 percent confident in your decision, the variability of life still exists. It's why no one can truly predict the weather.

Meteorologists have hundreds of data points and can give a fairly accurate prediction, but it's never 100 percent perfect. Have you heard of the butterfly effect? The hypothesis is that a butterfly flapping its wings could eventually lead to a typhoon. Instead of decisions being solely linear (2 + 3 = 5), there is always an element of unpredictability and variability. There are too many unknowns within the knowns for any prediction to be perfectly accurate.

I thrive on the illusion of being in control. If I have everything planned and under control and charted out, nothing bad can happen. But the more I seek out certainty, the more uncertain I actually become. Instead of coming up with solutions and a decision, I spend more time seeking out the potential downfalls. Trust me, you can always find out what won't work—especially if you're going for 100 percent certainty.

## Solution: Let Yourself Be Wrong

As a recovering perfectionist, this has been the hardest, most humbling part of my journey. I'm not great (okay, I'm terrible) at laughing at myself or my mistakes. I take mistakes personally, think they're a slam against me and my ability, and often get ridiculously defensive. Instead of allowing myself to be human, I expect perfection. So, to counter my own defensiveness, I allow myself to make decisions without knowing all the answers. I do my best. I allow myself to mess up and don't let it stop me from moving forward with peace.

Life is too short not to cut yourself a bit of slack. I want you to be okay with uncertainty, embrace the butterfly effect, and still make empowered decisions while igniting your spark.

## WELL, MAYBE . . .

The "how" to finding your spark involves two things: looking for your messages from the future and making decisions. The how isn't esoteric; it's in the mental work and in the audaciousness of no longer negotiating with yourself about how to find it and instead taking action and participating in finding it. Remember, you can adapt, you can adjust, you can learn, but you cannot do any of these things if you don't make at least one decision. If you're still stuck, let me offer one final way to help you narrow down options. Maybe you don't know exactly what to do but you do know what you *don't want* to do.

Dan and I have a Mastermind where we coach bloggers and entrepreneurs. Over the years we have come across clients who feel stuck and have no idea of the direction they want their platform to go or how to start. They are always worried and often will tell us how overwhelming and impossible it feels to have no direction. Then Dan will ask, "Do you want to write about Middle East oil companies?" Everyone (so far) has said no. They know immediately that they don't have interest in this space. Then Dan will ask them, "Do you want to write about moon-landing theories?" And again, so far, everyone has said no. Eventually, those who have no idea what they want to write about will find themselves narrowing down the field.

Sometimes the reason we're stuck is because we're trying to sift through *all* the possibilities. Start narrowing down the options until you get to a point where, just like our clients, instead of the immediate answer being, "No," the answer is, "Well, maybe . . ." coupled with the spark of hope. *Maybe* isn't no; *maybe* is you wondering if it might work.

Well, maybe I could write about parenting teens.
Well, maybe I could try that dance class.
Well, maybe I could reach out to the estranged friend.
Well, maybe I could start that blog.
Well, maybe I could go back to school.
Well, maybe I could . . .

Eventually, your "Well, maybe I could" will turn into a yes. Keep asking questions; keep daring to make decisions; keep taking small, positive action steps; and the "How do I find my spark?" will be replaced with a desire to keep it burning.

## FIRE STARTERS

Here are fifty *Message from the Future* questions designed to help you unearth your spark. The more honestly you answer, the more clarity will come.

1. Why do people come to you for advice?
2. What were you good at as a kid?
3. What did you give up doing in the last five years?
4. What did you give up doing in the last ten years?
5. What did you give up doing since you were a kid?
6. What are your regrets?
7. What's easy for you that amazes other people?
8. How do you like to relax?
9. What game show do you know you would do well at?
10. Are you a city, beach, or mountain person?
11. Are you outdoorsy or museum drawn?
12. Do you like country or rock and roll or classical music?
13. Do you have a green thumb?

14. Would you rather teach or take classes?

15. What is on your bookshelf now?

16. What book would you lend to a friend because it is *that* good?

17. Do you like photography?

18. Are you a writer?

19. What is in your keepsake box?

20. In your yearbook what were you "most likely" to do?

21. Do you have a degree that you haven't used?

22. What was your favorite elective in school?

23. What photos from your youth make you proud?

24. Do you have a dream board? If so, what's on it?

25. What do you love that others think is silly?

26. Did you like drama in school?

27. Can you play a musical instrument?

28. How do you decorate your home?

29. Do you love DIY, or do you hire out?

30. Have you made a bucket list? If so, what's on it?

31. What charity do you love helping?

32. What social media accounts do you follow?

33. What do you love to learn about?

34. Do you like animals?

35. Who inspires you?

36. When have you felt the happiest?

37. Where is your place of peace?

38. If money wasn't a barrier, where would you go?
39. If money wasn't a barrier, what would you do?
40. What do your kids see in you?
41. What song describes your life?
42. Who would you love to meet?
43. What makes you laugh?
44. If you had to give a speech unprepared, what could you talk about?
45. Where do you spend your free time?
46. When do you feel like the real you?
47. What five words would you use to describe yourself?
48. What would you do if you knew it would work out?
49. What do you love about you?
50. What is your message from the future?

Okay, the last one was a bit sneaky, but you get the point—you must start asking questions. You can't get to where you want to go by speeding along at a million miles an hour. You'll be going so fast that you'll miss the markers. In the notes you'll find a link to my website with more questions if you want to go deeper.[6]

# CHAPTER 5

# WHO AM I NOW?

## *Learning from Your Past and Letting Go*

In my closet is a pair of kelly-green shorts that I wore ten years ago. I'm pretty sure they're from Old Navy, and I'm also fairly sure that they're now terribly out of style. Or maybe they're back in style? I'm not a fashion blogger, so I don't know. I do know that those green shorts have had a hold on me. These were my "can I still fit into these?" shorts, a way I measured my worth. I'm sure you've got something like that in your life too. Maybe it's that dress you felt unstoppable in at your friend's wedding, or a pair of prepregnancy jeans, or the minivan you said you'd drive into the ground (you hate it but hang on to it to show your commitment to frugality). Most of us have something from the past that we measure our current life against.

Those ten-year-old green shorts have had the power to dictate my mood. If they were too tight, I'd be grumpy and anxious. If I could button them, I'd give myself a pat on my back (and probably eat an extra cookie). Those shorts have been like a sticky note on my rearview mirror that says, "If you can fit into these shorts, you are worthy."

What I haven't told you is that I bought those shorts when I was at my lowest weight—an unhealthy weight caused by the incredible stress from my separation and divorce. When I walked into Old Navy and bought them, my life was complex, stressful, and lonely. I had no appetite then. None. I was just trying to make it through. I lost so much weight that my friend Maria worried, and per her request, I went to the doctor to make sure I was okay. The doctor was worried but chalked it up to intense stress and told me to drink high-calorie protein drinks.

I'm not going to lie—I liked buying size-two shorts. I liked weighing what I had in high school. It gave me a sense of distorted power in a world that lacked control. As my life grew healthier, I regained some of the weight. I struggled with that too, as if something was wrong with me and I just needed to be more disciplined—versus realizing my body is considerably healthier now.

Those green shorts have been a central figure in my sense of self-confidence. They became an "ideal" of worth, a measuring stick for my value. Sometimes I need to remind my current self what size-two green-short-wearing Rachel hadn't yet done:

> ❯ She hadn't gone through a divorce, sat in a courtroom alone, and survived.
> ❯ She hadn't written three books and grown her social community to over a million.
> ❯ She hadn't dealt with the angst of estranged children and then mended the relationships.
> ❯ She hadn't moved a thousand miles from the home where she grew up with her kids.
> ❯ She hadn't discovered she was a strong and capable single mom.
> ❯ She hadn't appeared on national television or had her writing translated into over twenty-five languages.
> ❯ She hadn't graduated kids, filled out FAFSAs, and let them fly.
> ❯ She hadn't remarried and learned to trust and love again.
> ❯ She hadn't run eighty to one hundred miles per month, ran a half-marathon, and busted her limits.

> She hadn't taken care of her mental health, seen a counselor, or learned to deal with the past.
> She hadn't discovered her strength.
> She hadn't figured out just how brave she truly was.

That's what I've done since I bought those green shorts. And that list is a reminder for *me* as much as for anyone else that *the past does not determine your worth today*. Those green shorts no longer represent me, so why have I stayed so determined to fit into them?

What was the grip they had on me, and how do I let it go?

## RELEASING THE GRIP

My first clue that the green shorts didn't belong in my life anymore was the subtle realization that they were chipping away at my confidence. Instead of motivating, they discouraged. Instead of inspiring, they deflated. Instead of making me better, they made me feel less.

That's when I knew I needed to release their grip on my current identity.

As I considered how to take back my power, I questioned why these shorts even mattered to me. Was it truly the size? It might have been, but the real issue was deeper. While the size was a surface element, those shorts made me feel confident in a world where my confidence was constantly tested.

I didn't live in that intense confidence-testing world anymore, but the shorts kept me feeling as if I was. They didn't motivate me to become stronger; they only motivated me to try to fit into them. I'd go on a run and imagine coming home, going upstairs, trying them on, and them fitting. If they didn't fit when I got home, even after ten miles of running, I dismissed the stamina it had taken for me to complete that run and instead beat myself up.

This cycle finally ended when I went all in on my current story.

At a certain point on my soul's journey, I decided I might as well live life with everything I've got. I didn't want to live halfway, with regrets, or with fears that I wouldn't be able to handle something or that I would be seen as "too much." And as some of these changes started happening, I realized those green shorts didn't fit this new ethos. They didn't reflect my current values. They held me back, messed with my confidence, and pushed me to make choices that didn't fit who I was becoming.

So one day, after a run, I took a picture of those shorts on my closet floor, wrote an essay about my experience for my blog, and then decided never to try them on again. I took away their power by refusing to play the game any longer. I knew one thing: I didn't want to go back to being the person who fits into them again.

Do you have any items like this from your past? What are they? They could be clothing, memorabilia, family traditions, photos, you name it. What kind of a hold do they have on you? How do they make you feel? If you want to cut the tether, you need to come to grips, just like I did, that you might no longer fit whatever that item represents.

I had originally planned to donate the green shorts. But then I realized they are a powerful visual of the complexity of letting go and redefining self. So now they are in a box in my office, ready to be used as a visual during my speaking engagements.

Those green shorts are part of my story. They represent me—but the me from back then. They were worn by a brave soul who dared to say *enough* and change her life, who felt abandoned by many whom she thought were friends, who felt alone in her unraveling, and who survived.

These shorts belonged to a warrior. No wonder they had so much power. It just took me a minute to see that power—and it was far beyond being able to fit in them.

## FORGIVING YOURSELF

My counselor, Erika, helped me break free from burdens like my green shorts (she also first introduced me to the concept of residue). She never judged, never was impatient, but would lead me, question me, until the point that I'd have an aha moment and see the truth. During that process, it was important for me to be honest with myself about my wins, mistakes, and stumbling points. Without rigorous honesty, I couldn't have some of these realizations and then learn from them.

As we did this work together, she also taught me to forgive myself.

We can be our own worst enemy so often, can't we? I remember my mistakes, my errors, my fails and will use them as guideposts in life. Instead of positive guideposts, these negative guideposts would chip away at my confidence. When I came to a crossroads or needed to make a choice, my internal critic, which remembers the negative, would pipe up with, *Remember when you messed that up? Who's to say you won't again?* or *Remember how you put your hopes there? Let's not do that again. You might look foolish.*

This internal critic became my internal green-shorts marker—comparing stories rather than celebrating victories. The critic doesn't appreciate the tries; it only sees the fails. The critic lacks patience and wants results immediately. The critic refuses to give grace, only criticism.

Don't allow yourself to be your worst enemy by giving your internal critic undeserved power.

As I have worked through the process of silencing my inner critic, I've found a practice to be helpful. In a moment when my inner critic's voice is loud and I'm bombarded with memories of "failures," I will stop and whisper, "I forgive myself. I forgive my critic for holding me back."

The critic will tell you that grabbing the torch is pointless, not to look for your message markers, and most certainly will convince you that at times you just shouldn't care. The critic is both loud and a whisper of doubt. It takes diligence to discern those thoughts and feisty determination to redirect them to truth.

And you? You, too, get to choose if you give your internal critic any more power.

Does your internal critic even know who you are now? There's a good chance your inner critic hasn't caught up with where you are now. Mine looked at those green shorts and kept measuring me against them, against a goal that no longer fit who I was becoming. As I released myself from those old structures, I allowed my critic to evolve. And as time passed, I decided to reassign the critic's role altogether.

My critic has become my adviser, my right hand.

An adviser has your best interest at heart and looks for opportunities for you to excel. An adviser also confidently alerts you to situations, relationships, and thought patterns that might not be in your best interest. An adviser is there to support, build up, and assist. An adviser also asks the hard questions with your best interest at heart, including questions about green-shorts identities.

It's time you promoted your critic to adviser.

This process won't always be easy, but it will be worthwhile. It will require you to be aware of your inner dialogue instead of letting it just run freely. The critic doesn't have parameters to stop itself—it will continue to badger you—while the adviser wants you to be the best version of you that you can be. Many thoughts happen almost instantaneously, so be diligent in catching them. But also be gentle, because the critic is just the adviser misguided. Instead of cutting yourself down, be proud for stopping the thought patterns and changing them. Don't let critical thoughts take hold and plant roots.

I still worry, wonder, and question if I'll ever make it. But now, instead of letting those thoughts take hold, I forgive the thought and ask myself, *What's the truth?* The truth is that I can and I will make it. My journey might not be perfect, beautiful, or all put together, but with effort I can overcome, and I can do hard things.

You can too. You are working and committed, and you are worthy.

## WHEN LIFE IS CHALLENGING

The human experience is so complex—with tragedies, devastating moments, complicated experiences, loss, confusion, betrayal, intense stress, heartache . . . and so forth. I don't need to name the individual hardships we endure during our journey on this planet or explain why they're hard. If you're human, you're likely in the middle of some kind of life challenge right this minute or you've endured one. And if you're in the midst of heartbreak and tragedy, I want to acknowledge your strength in a space where you never wanted to be strong. I don't pretend to understand your pain, but I am holding space for you.

My previous financial ruin and subsequent divorce were areas where I carried a great deal of shame, especially in the years closest to it happening. I felt like I'd be walking through Target and people would be whispering, "You know she went through bankruptcy, right?" or "She signed divorce papers last week." Those moments were a challenge to my sense of identity for a long, long time.

Shame, anger, and bitterness can keep us from dreaming. They can tell us we're not worthy of a good life now. They remind us of the lows we felt and implore us to play it safe so that hardships never happen again. They discredit our bravery, minimize our potential, and chip away at our ability to trust. But the hard truth is this: no matter what we do now, those challenging and sometimes unfair events are always part of our stories and don't need to be held under the weight of shame, anger, and bitterness.

My youngest, Samuel, who's fourteen now, was diagnosed with celiac disease when he was a toddler (celiac disease is a chronic digestive and immune disorder, triggered by foods containing gluten, that damages the small intestine). He spent years with a compromised immune system and had his fair share of hospital stays.

When he was maybe four, he was at Minneapolis Children's Hospital for another lab draw. Samuel had already learned to hate labs, which meant I had to hold him down as he fought and cried for me to make them stop. In the beginning, I kept telling him, "It's okay, Samuel, it's okay." Then I realized: under no circumstance was this okay. Instead, I told him, "Samuel. This isn't fair. I'm sorry. It's not fair you have to deal with this. I'm here for you."

Life is full of not-fair moments.

My experience has been that it's good to recognize those hard moments instead of shoving them under the rug. The moment I told Samuel that I saw his unfair journey was when he had permission to deal with the challenges. Telling him it was okay minimized his reality versus acknowledging and respecting his journey. Ever since that day, he's been an advocate for his lab draw experience. He has learned to speak up, to ask for the butterfly needle, to tell them to wait until he's ready. Now, as a teenager, he handles his lab experience from start to finish. The technicians converse with him and he has taken control in the hard.

> Sure, things could be worse, but, friends, don't compare or judge someone's worst against yours. Have compassion and empathy. One of the worst things we can do as humans is to try to outpain[7] someone else.

I've learned a truth over the years that I hope might help you in dealing with your own unfair and challenging moments: your past doesn't need to constantly be in your future's line of sight. In other words, although I can't remove divorce, bankruptcy, or Samuel's celiac diagnosis from my history, I don't have to relive the intense emotions associated with those events daily.

These events are through lines in the timeline. They're not simply "a season" or a one-day shake-up; they are a part of our journey. Some events in our stories we simply can't "get over" or "forget" or "move on" from. They're too defining, too traumatic. But we can learn not to allow the charge of the event to maintain its intensity at every moment. It doesn't mean the event is erased, dismissed, fair, or okay. It doesn't mean we need to accelerate our timeline of healing to match what others think it should be. It doesn't mean we don't give ourselves space to grieve. It simply means that, with time, we get to a place where we allow ourselves to experience the good, the normal, and the joy in life too.

If you envision your timeline as a linear process, the events of the past would be on the left side of the line and your future to the right. There is chronological order—from A to B, from left to right. But some events, like tragedies and unexpected moments, can be pulled out of the order and held front and center. Sometimes they are there so we don't forget, and sometimes they are there because we don't know how to put them back in the timeline because we actually don't want to forget.

The best way I've learned to deal with the truly *nonlinear* process of grief and growth is to imagine a shelf in front of your timeline. On this shelf you can set out memories, like a book, that are important or defining. You can pick up the memory, look at it, experience the emotion, learn from it, but you also have the ability and choice to put it back on the shelf. When it's on the shelf, you aren't forgetting or denying it, but you're also not experiencing the full charge at every moment.

In the days after my separation, I didn't know how I'd survive or if the angst, sadness, and anxiousness would leave. Those were some of the longest days and months of my life. And while the divorce remains a through line in my story, the overwhelming emotion has subsided. As I healed, I also learned to tell my past that it didn't get to come with me into the future. It was no longer necessary for me to hold those emotions in my present. Past Rachel, when I was in the throes of the trauma, wanted normalcy and peace. So when present Rachel chooses to live fully, grateful for the normalcy of today, it is in some way honoring the Rachel who made it through and survived.

It also quickly became clear that I needed to guard myself against living with bitterness, shame, or anger. Those three emotions love to attach themselves to unfair and challenging events. Certainly, there are places in life when anger is justified, but if I spend twenty years being angry at my ex, I'm not allowing myself (or my ex) the freedom to grow and change. Anger is a tricky and valid emotion. We can be angry over situations, events, or the past, but we can't allow the anger to control us or determine our current outlook.

And bitterness and shame? Those two emotions keep our potential small and limited. Bitterness suffocates joy and tells us not to try again. Shame stifles courage and makes us believe we can never overcome what happened. All three of them can stand out on our life's timeline, and if we don't deal with them, they can smother our spark.

I believe a powerful antidote for anger, bitterness, and shame is gratitude.

This was never clearer than when Samuel was diagnosed with celiac disease. The only treatment for celiac is living with a strict gluten-free diet. Back in 2011, it wasn't as easy to get this diagnosis. It required a great deal of advocacy, sitting in hospital rooms, and the beginning of holding him down for yet another unpleasant test. And then a week after the biopsy and subsequent diagnosis, Samuel was back in the hospital, experiencing what turned out to be "celiac crisis," the body going into shock while adjusting to a gluten-free diet. Ironic, right?

We didn't know it was that upon admission, so numerous scary scenarios were being tossed around.

No one knew exactly why he was so ill, so we were in this miserable place of limbo. Around one in the morning, it was just Samuel and me in his room. I sat next to him, stroking his hair back from his face, and surprisingly felt grateful. Not fake, made-up gratitude but an authentic, deep gratitude in the midst of this challenge.

It started when I heard his heart-rate monitor keeping a perfect rhythm.

*Beep.*
*Beep.*
*Beep.*
*Beep.*
*Beep.*

As my tears fell, I became acutely aware of the parents in the hospital who would do anything for Samuel's normal heart rhythm. With that awareness came more gratitude: the IV in his arm that was getting him meds and fluids, nurses with colorful scrubs, gluten-free bread (which back then had the density of a rock), my cot, friends who brought coffee, extra cell-phone chargers left at the front desk, lab tests, and on and on. We were surrounded by care and gifts during this difficult time.

This is gratitude in the middle.

It didn't mean that what was going on was fair or that I was less frustrated and sad. It didn't mean I stopped advocating for him. It didn't mean celiac disease vanished. Instead, it was awareness that I could find joy (now you know even more about my blog's title) within the rough patches of life.

In these moments, the solution isn't just to power through but to also allow yourself to be human, to recognize the feelings, and to work through what might have been. Dealing with what might have been takes accepting feelings versus running from them. I've dealt with anger on my runs. Sometimes I physically pound it out on the pavement, and when the run is done, instead of packing up my anger to bring with me, I choose to let it go. Dealing with these emotions doesn't mean you magically make them disappear but rather that you don't allow the challenge to mire you in the negative. And then, as I learned, you dare to look for the gratitude within. Seeing the gratitude won't immediately change the situation, but it will change the intensity of the emotion.

## LETTING GO

Letting go isn't about forgetting. If anything, letting go is *honoring* your story, acknowledging the change in your hoped-for future, and daring to find joy and happiness in your present. Letting go allows you the emotional space to step into the next part of your story. Here are some ways I've dealt with letting go:

1. **Seek out support.** That might mean finding a counselor or perhaps it's a support group. Being vulnerable in this setting will allow you to address the green-shorts markers in your life, your inner critic, and shame you don't need to carry. That vulnerability can also inspire profound confidence. It takes confidence to deal with the past instead of bury it. It takes confidence to forgive. It takes confidence to find gratitude too—especially when the road is hard.

2. **Pursue forgiveness.** This might mean making amends, asking for forgiveness, forgiving others, as well as forgiving yourself. We can be really hard on ourselves and punish ourselves for past mistakes. You are worth forgiving the past you. Forgiveness takes practice, and it's rarely a one-time act. Forgiving doesn't mean you forget; rather, forgiveness allows you to move on, untethered from the angst of the past. When you forgive, you regain control of your timeline's perspective.

3. **Be open to learning.** Instead of judging yourself harshly, the way the inner critic is known to, listen to the voice of the adviser, who asks, "Is there anything you can learn from this situation?" And then be open to that honest guidance. You might hear insights that are uncomfortable. Instead of running from that feedback, lean in and try to get to the deeper meaning. Learning also stops you from ruminating on the past. Learning invites you to come up with a solution and the courage to accept your story.

4. **Stay present.** Even though we are on a journey to get your spark back, I need you to stay present in the journey too. You can't go back and change the past; you can only do the work now to change the future. But that also means that the time in front of you is just as valuable. Letting go, forgiving, accepting, and learning will allow you to love yourself for who you are now. It will cause you to celebrate the little moments, the successes, and to be grateful for opportunity.

When I was in college, I had a studio arts class where the professor would have everyone put their projects on the wall—just like grade school, but this was an honors design class. Once we all tacked our projects up, for the next hour, we'd take turns discussing them.

I quickly learned that if I wanted to improve in that class, I had to be okay with both the negative and the positive feedback. If students were stubborn and defended everything they had done, they didn't grow or innovate as quickly. The most innovative moments happened when a student would listen to a critique without taking it personally. Then, the process became a collaboration, a sharing of ideas—and the outcome was often far superior.

I don't remember much else about that art class. But that lesson alone has stuck with me ever since and has shaped how I receive feedback. Oftentimes, I'm more grateful for those in my life who can say, "Have you thought about it this way instead?" It doesn't mean I'm wrong. It's just another option, another way of seeing, and having an open spirit has resulted in so much growth.

I want you to remember that *you are in charge* of your response now. You are responsible for your choices in this moment. You are responsible for dealing with your past too. And don't forget: there are some things you no longer need to take with you.

Give yourself the grace to allow yourself to move to the next chapter in life.

## FIRE STARTERS

✦ **Be willing to part with your "green shorts."** You might not be in the same spot you once were. You might not fit the degree you went to college for or love what you once loved. You don't have to do what you've grown out of loving. There is no hard-and-fast rule that you can choose only one path in life. I think of midlife (and all the unexpected moments) as a recalibration. Just because you loved something when you were twenty doesn't mean you have to love it at fifty. Life is a constant journey of recalibrating, adding in, and letting go. The hardest part of letting go is learning to appreciate the you of the past . . . and then letting yourself move forward. Applaud the woman who got you here. And remember, the woman who got you here wouldn't want who you are now to hold back.

✦ **Decide what to keep and what to let go.** So what do you do with physical relics from the past? I kept some that motivated or inspired me. But any reminders that kept me feeling small, I let go. When I was moving from Minnesota to Tennessee, I found a box of journals from the darkest of times in my previous marriage. Intrigued, I started reading, but the sadness in those words was hard to deal with. I ultimately decided to throw them away. "But what if there was something brilliant in there?" you might be asking. I couldn't risk reading them—they were too hard, too triggering. I needed to let them go so I could be free. Examine whether reminders from the past are helping or hurting you, and be willing to make bold choices for your future benefit.

✦ **Allow your kids to let go too.** One of the greatest gifts you can give adult kids is to allow them to throw away items from their past. I saved what I thought was important for my older kids and shipped it to them with a note that said, "I love you. I saved these papers, trinkets, and stuff from your childhood. It might not have the same meaning for you, and that is okay. Feel free to get rid of anything in here. It won't hurt my feelings."

# CHAPTER 6

# WHAT IF I'M REJECTED?

## The Paradox of Caring

My son Caleb is an avid Goodwill shopper. He'll visit our Goodwill several times a month, and on most of our family trips his stop of choice will be the local Goodwill. I confess that I don't have the patience to thumb through rack after rack of clothing to find a diamond-in-the-rough shirt like he does. Throughout high school, Caleb developed his own unique and quirky style. Most of the time, his style didn't make sense to me, so I'd buy him something from Old Navy—only to see it sit in his closet with the tags still attached.

For many years, I'd think, *You're wearing that?* Some days I'd even voice it—only to be met with the teenager response of, "Uh, why? Is there a problem?" I worried that he wouldn't fit in or he'd be made fun of for clothing choices I didn't understand.

Then, at senior awards night, Caleb was voted "Best Dressed Male" by his entire class. Caleb's style had evolved, and others would comment about how he dressed so cool. Still, the award surprised me! And then I thought about it—Caleb cared more about his own style than he did about fitting in and dressing in the "acceptable" style, and as a result, he stood out. He was seen in a world of sameness. When Caleb was younger, kids would tease him, but that didn't make him pull the jeans from Old Navy out of the closet and rip off the tags. He kept following his heart, his style, and on that muggy May evening, his authenticity was rewarded.

I wouldn't have had the guts to be as bold as Caleb when I was in high school. I either fit in, or I stood out and was picked on, which meant I spent more time caring about the opinions of others instead of caring about figuring myself out. Caring became linear, black and white, either-or, and there wasn't much wiggle room.

Caring requires both-and thinking. Both-and thinking is a newer philosophical approach to decision-making that isn't rooted in either-or determinations (also known as *dualistic thinking*). Either-or thinking is binary and results in two outcomes. Either you win *or* you lose.

Either you succeed *or* you fail. Either you have friends *or* you are alone. Either I'm right and you're wrong *or* you're right and I'm wrong. Either you wear the trendy clothes *or* you're picked on.

By design, either-or thinking has been essential to the decision-making that has led to many of the technological, medical, and industrial advances in our lives. There are also times when dualistic thinking is critical—either you stop at the stop sign and prevent an accident *or* you blow right through and cause an accident.

This thinking is rooted in choosing one or the other—there is no in-between. Back when I decided I wanted to go all in on my life, I knew I needed to make a strong, unbreakable decision, one that I couldn't back out of. Either-or thinking is what it looks like to go all in on your life. You care so much about *you* that you either pursue this or you don't—no middle ground. You don't cut corners and give yourself a pass. Either you set and complete goals *or* you don't.

Even with all the benefits of either-or thinking, it can limit our ability to see the nuances in life, the spaces in between, especially in the creative and entrepreneurial processes. A decision needs to be made, but there also needs to be room to adjust the decision or see new possibilities. I call this the *paradox of caring*.

Aerospace engineer Jeffrey Bolognese's description of the paradox of light can inform our approach to caring:

> Up until the beginning of the 20th century, science held an *either/or* understanding of the nature of light. Some scientists believed light was a particle because it demonstrated characteristics of a particle. Others said light must be a wave, because it demonstrated the characteristics of a wave. Experiments could be conducted that demonstrated either of those views. However, neither of those theories alone could fully explain the behavior of light. It took the radical notion that light could be both a wave and a particle for a more complete understanding.
>
> That *both/and* view not only gave us insight into light, but opened up the study of quantum physics. And, of course, without quantum physics you wouldn't have that computer or smart phone you're using right now to read this fine article.
>
> In that case, *both/and* thinking allowed for a change in our fundamental understanding of the universe. While most of our decisions don't have such ramifications, when we apply *both/and*

thinking to our decision-making process, we open up many more possibilities.[8]

This both-and approach to how much we care about something demonstrates the paradox of caring—you need to *both* care about your life, your heart, the hard things *and* not so care so much about what others think. You can *both* care about being a good human *and* not care if others see you as a good human. You can *both* care about going all in on your life *and* not care if others question your life choices.

I'm not using the concept of "not caring" as meaning that you can be a jerk and cut someone off on the way to church or the grocery store. Not caring means that you refuse to allow someone else's actions or words to dictate your response or influence your identity. If someone cuts *you* off, you choose to not take it personally and you also don't ride their tail in a fit of road rage (chances are, that guy will be waved into the parking spot next to you at church (or buying bananas next to you at Kroger). Not caring means you don't allow another's external choices to define your internal worth. The guy who cut you off might have had a valid reason (or maybe not), but you don't have to care enough to create a hypothetical reason to allow that experience to trickle into the rest of your day or to be a commentary on your identity.

The person in the car doesn't have the authority to override your identity. However, when our caring paradox is out of balance, those outside acts can make us vulnerable to accepting the actions (or words) of others as truth about ourselves. Even though people teased Caleb for years about his Goodwill style, he didn't allow their words to chip away at his identity.

Caring is a *both-and* situation—with a need to both care deeply and also care less. See the paradox? You need to both care enough to continue to say yes to yourself, which might make waves, and also to not care about what people might be saying about said waves.

The waves, by the way, aren't a negative outcome of change. They're just the visible outcome. People talk about whatever is happening (or about you) because it's something they see, which can make them wonder, *Do I need to make waves?* or *Why is my life the way it is?* And sometimes, after a while, the person who created the waves ends up being seen and rewarded for not caring that they made the waves. I know because there is a little gold plastic statue in my home honoring my best-dressed boy, who didn't care if he made waves and looked different.

## WHY DO YOU CARE?

Have you seen the episode *Friends* where Rachel and Phoebe decide to start running in Central Park? Rachel runs how I *hope* I run—composed, with a good stride, and confident. Phoebe, on the other hand, runs without rules—legs flailing, arms all over the place, laughing the entire time. At first, Rachel is mortified by Phoebe's "style" and boldly remarks how she can't be seen running with her. Rachel's reason? She disliked that others were looking at them like they were quite strange.

"Why do you care?" Phoebe responds.

"Because they're people!" Rachel says.[9]

Ouch. How often do we care so much about the opinions of people who might see us stepping outside the expected that we douse that spark that made us want to try in the first place? Probably far too often. We care because if someone says something, it means they've been observing us and coming to conclusions, and that person's potential criticism can feel like a big warning for us to get back in line so we don't look like what society might deem as foolish.

No one has it all together. But we inherently care so much about other people *thinking* we have it all together.

This collective caring results in a culture of people constantly trying to act like we have it together to avoid attention or impress others—because underneath, we're afraid we're not enough. But enough for whom? What? No matter how much television, social media, influencers, and others may try to convince you that you need to be thinner, healthier, and wealthier in order to be happier or find your spark, none of those things truly matter when it comes as an expectation from others. And there is nothing wrong with wanting to have it together—except that often it means we care too much about what others think and not enough about what we think. We sacrifice our authenticity to fit in, or we adopt a lifestyle that doesn't fit our ethos.

Phoebe ran that way because it was fun and free, a lot like how a little kid runs. She didn't care what people thought and even told Rachel that the opinions of the people Rachel was so worried about were people they would never see again. How many times have you not done something because you were worried others might see you? And is it really about seeing you? Or is it about seeing you not at your best? Is it about not fitting in?

And therein lies the caring paradox—we care about a lot (people, events, etc.), but we get to decide *what* and *who* has power over our emotional state. Phoebe wasn't a robot. She cared about things! She cared about running and cared about Rachel's opinion of her running. She didn't like that Rachel was embarrassed by her running style. Now, even though Rachel's opinion of her bothered her, she kept running her way. She didn't care what random people in Central Park thought. In other words, she didn't give strangers the same amount of weight in the caring paradox as she gave to Rachel.

You can't go through life caring about everything. You'd be crushed if every honk, flipped bird, evil look, teenage sigh, or grumbling from strangers had that much power. If you take stuff personally, you're making it about you, not the other person. Let's revisit our road rage example. Say you make a bone-headed move on the road. Another driver honks at you, probably to warn you to stop or watch out.

Most likely, the other driver isn't cutting you down as a person. They may be ticked off by your driving, but they're not judging you personally. And even if they're the biggest jerk in the world and are bashing you for making a mistake, *you still don't have to care*. You don't have to take it as a commentary on your worth. You can (and should) care enough to fix your driving but not enough that their words about you remain part of your identity.

Just not caring sounds like it should be easy, right? But we humans make it complex. Let's say you stop at

Starbucks before a critical work meeting. Not only is it busy, but they changed the menu boards. Again. You're trying something new (because you're stepping outside your box), so you ask the barista, "What's awesome?" The barista begins asking what you like and sharing about their newest ice drink. Well, the gal behind you is in a rush and makes a snarky comment about how long it's taking, and then the guy behind her chuckles in agreement. You're annoyed and a bit embarrassed.

Do you allow this random interaction with a random person to cut away or chip at your confidence or your mood? Are you slamming your $6.55 iced latte and God-forbid spilling some of that precious elixir on your desk later? Are you complaining about it at the water cooler?

That's caring in the wrong space.

Let's say your best friend is in the car with you and points out that you missed a stop sign. You'd care what she says because she cares about you and your safety. If your spouse comes to you and says he's worried because you've been a bit short-tempered with the kids, you'd likely listen—because you want to interact positively with your kids.

The paradox of caring can be resolved when you delineate what is worth caring about versus what is worth letting go.

## PROTECTING YOUR EMOTIONAL RESERVE

Remember the adviser versus the critic? The adviser will give you info; the critic will take it as a slam on self.

Caring gets messy when we allow all events to have the same effect on our psyche. If the stranger who flipped you the bird or grumbled at your Starbucks experience can affect your mood as much as your best friend talking to you about needing to let go of a past hurt, more than likely you haven't developed a strategy for what you allow to affect you and for how long.

*In a quest to understand the paradox more, I asked someone who beautifully lives out this duality (to be both caring and not caring) about his strategy: my husband, Dan.*

*Dan is friends with pretty much everyone. He knows all the cashiers at Kroger and most of our neighbors, and he has a ridiculously large digital Rolodex of connections. People who have met Dan know one thing about him: he shows up. Whether it's helping our neighbor Jason build a basketball half-court in his backyard or hauling groceries in for another neighbor, Dan will be there. He cares a ton about helping people. But he also does (and says) what he wants. You might think he doesn't care about social norms or keeping the status quo, and while there is an element of truth in that, Dan really cares about his heart and his family.*

*He will say the hard things instead of sugarcoating them to make others comfortable. Dan would run like Phoebe and laugh and have a great time and not worry what anyone thought. He will take on projects that others might say are too hard or too risky, but because he has the inner drive, he won't let their words or worry stop him.*

*Dan's strategy? He knows his heart, his capabilities, and he loves who he is and his family. That's the caring fence for him. Anything outside of that boundary doesn't necessarily affect his mood or capabilities. He might have a moment when he's annoyed at someone who rejects an idea. He'll even assess whether the idea has merit. But ultimately, Dan chooses to do what he needs to do.*

Your strategy for deciding what is worth expending your emotional energy on won't be exactly like Dan's, and it shouldn't. You know your limits and the boundaries where you need to put down your foot and the areas that are worth letting slide in order to protect your peace.

Protecting your peace is a form of caring. It's different than avoidance. It's the boundary you've created that others don't get to cross.

Caring can get messy when the people you care most about don't agree with the path you're on. It might be your folks, your partner, your kids, your coworkers, or your best friend. When they aren't on board with your choices or boundaries, it can feel like you're disappointing others, which might cause you to back down in order to avoid upsetting the balance. It's a difficult balance of learning to hear the perspectives of those you trust but also being able to call on your inner wisdom to stand up for your choices. Respect your perspective enough to create your own caring boundary.

For decades, we've heard about the importance of boundaries, yet the work of actually establishing those boundaries often takes a backseat. Boundaries can be tricky because while they protect *us*, they affect the lives of others. We can't assume that others, especially family or friends, will agree with every boundary we set. We can adapt and learn (both-and), but at a certain point, our boundaries need some rigidity—otherwise they're just suggestions, not boundaries. A caring boundary could be as simple as Sunday is family day or as complex as turning down invitations that don't align with your beliefs.

Later in the *Friends* episode, Rachel is doing her normal not-bringing-attention-to-herself safe run. As she stops to catch her breath, she looks around, shrugs her shoulders, and starts to run Phoebe's free run. With flapping and flailing arms, she and Phoebe (who was also running) cross paths.

"You're right! This feels great!" Rachel exclaims.

"See?" Phoebe responds. "And you don't care if people are staring because it's just for a second and then you're *gone!*"[10]

## THE FREEDOM TO BE YOURSELF

When I was in third grade, it was the height of the Cabbage Patch craze. This was the era of stampedes and brawls in stores over a doll with fancy adoption papers. Despite the craze, I have never owned one. I've never asked my parents why I didn't get one, but I also didn't really care that much—until the Cabbage Patch birthday party incident. The party was on a Saturday in May, and we were told to dress up for a tea party and to bring our Cabbage Patch dolls with their adoption papers so we could share stories. The presupposition was that we all had this famous eighties icon.

That was one of the first times I remember caring about fitting in . . . and realizing I didn't.

My never-back-down mom found one of her old dolls, made it an outfit, and got it ready for the party. She told me the doll didn't matter and that I should be proud. I walked into the party with this doll, which unlike a Cabbage Patch doll was stiff and didn't bend, proud that it was once my mom's. The party was uncomfortable, and on that day I adopted two inaccurate caring beliefs: that I needed to care enough to fit in, and that I needed to care enough to make others happy.

We all gathered in the wood-paneled family room and shared adoption papers. I didn't have adoption papers, just the story that my doll once was my mom's, and several of the girls began to comment on that with loud-enough-to-be heard whispers and eye rolls. I remember sitting in my chair and taking their words so personally, as if something was wrong with me for not having a Cabbage Patch doll. That was the moment I thought, *You must care enough to fit in, or else you will be teased.*

There's a picture of this party somewhere in the childhood memorabilia my mother has saved. In this picture, the party participants are all standing in front of a pond, holding our dolls. Although little Rachel is smiling, adult Rachel can see the sting of rejection in my young eyes. I smiled for my mom so she wouldn't be hurt, but behind the smile I was embarrassed and heartbroken.

That event had a bunch of caring moments all pushed together. First, I didn't want to hurt my mom's feelings— my mom who cared enough to spend time getting the doll ready for the party. I remember not wanting to make a fuss about not having the Cabbage Patch doll and relenting to bring the other doll.

Second, I don't think I was ready for the level of drama that me not having the right doll created. Instead of my doll just being accepted, I was singled out and made fun of—and not just by anyone but by girls I considered my friends. At that age, I didn't have the skills to cope with that.

Third, I didn't know how to handle the complex and dichotomous emotions this situation brought about all the caring stuff—the pressure of not wanting to hurt my mom while also being hurt myself—so instead of caring, it was the first time I remember saying, "I don't care."

But I did care. I was hurt. I said I didn't care as an act of defense, as if I could trick my heart into not caring and deflect the attention of others. I really did care, and the proud, independent part of me flickered. Instead of confidently being me, I became deflated. That moment, at such a formative age (I clearly still remember the details of that day all these years later), taught me to believe that it was risky to stand out, risky to run with my arms flapping, risky to show up differently—because not only would I be seen, but I might also be rejected.

At some point, most of us learn to care about other people so we don't have to deal with the pain of being rejected. Instead of rejection having a caring boundary (strangers or friends or family)—we allow it to define our worth and abilities. Rejection cuts deep. It unearths primal thoughts, *What is wrong with me?* Rejection makes us take those negative statements and thoughts inward versus examining the outward influence.

And we learn, just like I did in that moment, that we don't want to look foolish in front of others, so we work to stay within the bounds of what we think is acceptable. We don't want to rock the boat, so we try to keep the status quo. We don't want to be judged, so we minimize our dreams. The result? We find ourselves letting people walk past our boundaries; we shy away from doing the hard or different thing; we live life as if we aren't in control.

What about you? I'm sure you've experienced moments like mine when your spirit had a box of rejection thrown on it. And if you were young, without the resources and mindset tools you have now, that rejection likely made a deep wound and could be the unconscious reason why you might ration your emotions to care more about fitting in versus standing out or being yourself. Perhaps instead of expanding who you are, you shrink to fit in. You decorate with trendy colors even if you don't like them so your home matches your friends'. You learn not to ask questions because at some point your questions were made fun of.

Many of us stop caring in hopes that we can avoid others' criticism of our dreams or cutting down our progress or laughing at our stumbles. Instead of creating boundaries about what to care about, we tell ourselves we need to constantly worry about fitting in, to be aware of when we don't, and to be ready to justify and explain when we diverge from the norm.

The paradox of caring is the tension found within both either-or and both-and. You need both. You need to absolutely care and to care so much about your own heart that you go all in. But you also need to not care about the hypothetical views others might have about you going all in.

◪ ✦ ◪

The moment you realize how much you want the freedom to be yourself is the moment you finally give oxygen to your soul's dreams. Until you can acknowledge that you've kept yourself small in some ways, that you've avoided boundaries to the detriment of your dreams, all under the guise of caring about others' opinions, you will miss out on opportunities.

Care enough about you. Don't fear rejection! When you care so much about not being rejected by others, you are, in some ways, rejecting yourself. Fear rejecting yourself, abandoning yourself, more than you fear the rejection of others. Your soul needs you to care about you.

If you are living from a place of healthy boundaries and honest intentions and humility, whatever you choose to pursue will bring with it possibility and hope. You can follow rules and still speak up when the rules discriminate. You can be rejected and still realize that rejection doesn't define you. You can reframe caring.

You can run like Phoebe, carry your own doll, dress like Caleb, and not care what anyone thinks. You are dynamic! You are worth being your own quirky, wonderful, authentic, fabulous self.

Don't let the opinions of others box in the spark that is you.

## FIRE STARTERS

✦ **Care enough to try.** And then be okay with uncertainty. Caring doesn't mean you can control the outcome. That might mean someone laughs at you as you run like Phoebe through Central Park. Can you survive that? Absolutely. In the next week, find something that you've put off and try it.

Maybe it's meeting with a friend or going through the big pile of mail on your desk. Once, when I was still dealing with creditors, I was freaked out about calling about my student loan because I was afraid they'd judge me. I realized I cared more about being judged than fixing the situation. When I understood how out of order I had this, I made the call, and to my surprise the individual on the other line was grateful (and proud) that I had taken the step to call. Instead of judging me, they went out of their way to help.

+ **Care enough to take care of yourself.** Get adequate sleep; eat healthy; take care of your mind (again, why I meditate). If you're depleted, others' critiques or opinions will have a higher chance of sticking. But if you're mentally strong, you'll have the capacity to identify what is actually helpful and then say, "Nope. Not today." And care enough to have fun! Create moments of fun in your day, times when you laugh, times when you feel carefree. Laughter is a beautiful way to invest in your soul.

+ **Create a hierarchy of importance.** I tend to over-care or spread my caring too thin. I once was the person going into a meeting with thirteen "pressing" issues to address. Because my list was so long, none would get resolved. To address this, I created a hierarchy of importance for caring. If I were to attend that hypothetical meeting now, most items on that list would be relegated to "not that big a deal" so we

156

could focus on priorities. If you get bogged down in caring about every minor thing, when you bring up big issues, your voice may be diluted by too many prior instances of not identifying what was really important.

✦ **Differentiate between caring and worrying.** Worrying eats away at our time as we mull over what might/could/should/didn't happen. Worrying may *feel* like you're caring, but if you're not seeking a solution and are instead fixating on what-ifs, it's best to table that topic and stop worrying. Care about the situations and responses you have control over.

# CHAPTER 7

# HOW DO I START?

## *Reap the Rewards of Being a Beginner*

When my kids were young, they loved *The Magic School Bus*. *The Magic School Bus* was first a series of books designed to get kids excited about science topics. After that, it became a cartoon series on PBS. Many afternoons, I'd watch alongside them as Ms. Frizzle, the eccentric science teacher with the fabulous science-inspired outfit, would take the class on field trips. They weren't your typical go-to-the-zoo field trips; these field trips were pure science magic.

Within seconds of loading onto the bus, that magical school bus would transform into part of the latest science topic. If they were studying the water cycle, the bus (and the kids) would become raindrops. If they were learning about the human body, they'd be swallowed and would journey down the esophagus, into the stomach, and through the intestinal tract. If the lesson was about bugs, they'd become a butterfly—in all its life stages. *The Magic School Bus* brought science to life, and instead of memorizing science facts, kids were given permission to imagine. At some point during every episode, Ms. Frizzle would tell her class, "Take chances! Make mistakes! Get messy!"

Do you know what Ms. Frizzle was really saying?

*Be a beginner.*

Kids, of course, have permission to be beginners. After all, they're at the beginning of life with more than likely a lengthy timeline ahead of them. Adults, on the other hand, typically operate under a different set of expectations. There comes a day, for adults, when Ms. Frizzle's words move from adventurous to risky. Being a beginner in midlife is deemed no longer practical and doesn't fit the propaganda of planning for a retirement.

But I'm here to help you shift that thinking. You can be a beginner at any age!

## SAY YES

Folded in my dresser is a black T-shirt with a red CFMC across the chest and on the back a weight bench with the words *Cross Fit Music City*. That shirt was part of the "thank you for signing up for our six-week (dare we say it will be hard) challenge" that Dan and I joined in 2019. I knew, after a tour of the facility, that we'd be interacting with a super fit, energetic, "if I can do it, so can you" coach.

In one of the rooms was the body scan machine. It's like a scale on steroids that spits out not only measures of weight but also hydration, fat, and muscle in the body. As techie as I am, I hate the scale part. (This goes back to the green-shorts struggle, and now that I've identified that, I remember to remind myself that numbers don't matter.) After the scan is complete, the coach sets a hard but doable goal, we sign some papers, and then we take a couple *before* pictures.

As much as I dislike taking a before picture, I know it's critical for reframing success. Change is micro, day by day, and just as you don't see your kid go instantly from four feet to six feet (remember the first- and last-day-of-school pics), you don't see the process of change in yourself unless you have some frame of reference to start from.

Our neighbor Jason has been working on a massive backyard project over the last eighteen months. What once was a hill with potential is now a basketball *half-court, fire pit, and awesome outdoor kitchen. Last week, he told us he wished he had a time-lapse of the process because it's easy to forget the before as well as all the steps in between.*

After the enrollment process, the torch is passed to the clients: show up, do the work, try, don't quit, push your limits.

I wasn't on an island in CrossFit. But it was all new—me, in a gym, trying to figure out pretty much everything. I had *never* been to a gym, *never* lifted a heavy bar over my head, and *never* climbed a giant rope suspended from the rafters.

*But here's the thing:* **never** *ends the moment you say yes.*

Gradually, I picked up on what to do. I learned that I loved the rowing machine and hated the big medicine balls they want you to squat with and then throw high onto a wall just to catch again . . . and repeat. That right there—throwing a fifteen-pound ball higher than a line on a wall—was hell on earth. I kept doing them, though. I never grew to like it, but I put in the work because I made a commitment to complete the challenge.

When we signed up, I had zero clue what I was getting myself into beyond what I've seen on the website and in the twenty minutes I wandered the gym. I felt a kinship with the *Survivor* contestants who tell the camera, "When you're watching at home, this experience seems like one thing, but when you get out here? It's real. And it's much harder than I expected." Some mornings I didn't know if I'd be able to get through the workout. And then when I did, the sense of accomplishment motivated me to come back two days later and do it again.

My biggest mental hurdle during that very first CrossFit experience wasn't the scale. It wasn't the workout itself. The biggest hurdle was being uncomfortable with not knowing what to do or how it all worked! I don't like being a beginner. At all. In those initial sessions, I would have preferred the misery of throwing a medicine ball on the wall over the vulnerability of being a beginner. But despite my beginner anxiety, I kept walking through the door into the gym, determined not to let anything hold me back.

Where does this beginner fear come from? For me, it was rooted in years of bullying. Kids can be mean and cruel and can say some nasty stuff to other kids. When you're bullied, you make a choice: stand up to the bullies or tolerate them. I discovered quickly that I was terrible at standing up to the bullying. I'd cry almost immediately, which is the kiss of death for a bullied kid. So I tried to tolerate or ignore it, which meant I ultimately absorbed all the bullying, stuffed the feelings inside, and worked hard not to make a scene. That was my coping strategy. I wasn't ignoring it. I just wasn't fighting back. I wasn't thinking that what they said wasn't true. I accepted it as truth. I learned to stay under the radar in hopes that they might not see me.

Being a beginner can feel a lot like making a scene, like all eyes are on you.

Most of us don't like being the beginner or the new kid. Those moments can feel like the world is watching us and whispering about our beginner status. But if we don't push through the beginner sludge, we prevent ourselves from trying new, amazing, and fabulous things.

I worked for years to dissect the root of my fear of being a beginner. I discovered it was linked to not wanting to be rejected (the caring game) and keeping myself under the radar (raise the bar limits), all in hopes of not getting hurt. Bullying hurts, especially when you haven't learned how not to absorb the meanness or take it as an indicator of worth. I spent way too many years wrongly assuming that bullying was about who I was and that I needed to change.

Ignoring was the strategy of an awkward preteen and teenager, and I didn't want to carry that outdated mode of operation into my present. So now, instead of avoiding uncomfortable situations where I might be a beginner, I intentionally put myself into them. Then, in the moments of nervousness, I tell myself, "You are not thirteen anymore. You are an adult, and you are worthy of trying."

## REFRAME YOUR FEARS

On that first worry-filled morning at CrossFit, Dan, who was also a beginner, heard my giant list of reasons why I shouldn't go through the gym doors. But he didn't indulge my fears. He listened, then asked, "Are you ready to go in?" At times, voicing worries in a safe space can help to diffuse the intensity of the worry. If you don't have a friend to talk to, just speak them out loud to yourself or write them down. When you hear the worry, often you can rebut your own fear.

For reference, here is a short list of my first-morning worries:

> *The other people will see me mess up.*
> *They're going to judge me.*
> *I shouldn't have worn these shoes.*
> *What if I throw up?*

> ❯ *What if the other people talk about me?*
> ❯ *How do I put the weights on/off?*
> ❯ *How do I get my body to do that?*
> ❯ *What if I can't finish?*

If I had let those worries win, I might not be able to proudly wear my CFMC shirt. Instead of sinking into the fears, I reframed them. When you reframe a limit or belief, you are pulling out the presupposition you believe to be true and replacing it with the actual truth. A reframe is nonemotional and logically based and can disempower fears that might linger.

The simplest way to create a reframe is to ask a question regarding a presupposition or assumption in the original statement or question. For example, if I said, "Bethany lost her keys again," the presupposition might be that Bethany loses her keys regularly. I'd likely assume that Bethany chronically loses her keys, but it just as easily could be that this is only the second time she's lost them. The best thing I could do is *ask questions*. Assumptions can lead you down a road that isn't true, which is why asking the clarifying questions is critical.

Here's the same first-day worry list with the reframe questions:

> *The other people will see me mess up.*
> — Why do you assume you'll mess up? Why do you assume others will be watching you?
> *They're going to judge me.*
> — Why do you assume they are the judging type? Why do you care if they judge?
> *I shouldn't have worn these shoes.*
> — How could you have known what shoes to wear?
> *What if I throw up?*
> — Can you survive throwing up? Why do you think you might throw up?
> *What if the other people talk about me?*
> — Again, why are you assuming they'll talk about you instead of encouraging you?
> *How do I put the weights on/off?*
> — Do you think you won't be able to figure it out? What if someone offers to help you?
> *How do I get my body to do that?*
> — Isn't that why you're here? Why do you think you have to be perfect at this the first time?
> *What if I can't finish?*
> — What if you *can* finish? What would happen if you didn't finish?

Now, let's take it one step further—the same initial questions, the reframe questions, and then the worry reframed.

> *The other people will see me mess up.*
>   — Why do you assume you'll mess up? Why do you assume others will be watching you?
>     • *I will do my best and be supported.*
> *They're going to judge me.*
>   — Why do you assume they are the judging type? Why do you care if they judge?
>     • *I don't care what people say, because I am capable.*
> *I shouldn't have worn these shoes.*
>   — How could you have known what shoes to wear?
>     • *I am wearing the shoes I need to succeed today.*
> *What if I throw up?*
>   — Can you survive throwing up? Why do you think you might throw up?
>     • *I can survive challenging myself and getting sick.*
> *What if the other people talk about me?*

> — Again, why are you assuming they'll talk about you instead of encouraging you?
>> • *I can be happy and strong despite negative feedback.*

> *How do I put the weights on/off?*
>> — Do you think you won't be able to figure it out? What if someone offers to help you?
>>> • *I can figure things out, and if I need help, I am comfortable asking.*

> *How do I get my body to do that?*
>> — Isn't that why you're here? Why do you think you have to be perfect at this the first time?
>>> • *I am strong and can learn to do new things.*

> *What if I can't finish?*
>> — What if you *can* finish? What would happen if you didn't finish?
>>> • *I can finish hard things. My track record for surviving my worst day is 100 percent. And if I can't finish, I can try again next time.*

Over the years, I've kept a reframe journal. I'll write the reframes and put them in places where I can easily see them as regular reminders. If being a beginner is uncomfortable for you as well, make your own reframe list. I've lived with regret over allowing my fear of being a beginner to stop me from accepting jobs, pursuing opportunities, and even taking a chance to study at an ultra-cool college of architecture in California because I listened to the voice of fear. I don't want that for you! I want you to confidently step into new things, proud of being the beginner no matter where you are starting from or how old you are.

Thousands of years of survival has made humans' flight-fight-freeze-or-fawn response easily triggered. While that response is critical if you've just avoided a car wreck, it isn't essential if you're trying to avoid doing the clean jerk at CrossFit, or speaking up in a meeting where you're usually quiet, or meeting with the loan officer who is helping you refinance, or are singing a solo at church. Despite the lengthy multipage waiver you're required to sign, the probability is exceptionally high that attending CrossFit won't kill you, speaking up is needed, the loan officer is trying to help you, and singing in church is awesome! However, our brains, when put into new scenarios, aren't always good at distinguishing between real threats (a tiger charging you) and perceived threats (lifting a heavy bar in front of fifteen other people). Our responses can get all mixed up, and that rush of adrenaline, worry, or panic sets in and crowds out the real truth—it's just a bar, and if you can't lift it, you will survive.

When you don't deal with your fears, your fears will deal with you. Many fears can be traced back to events that no longer have bearing on who we are now. My midforties self doesn't need her thirteen-year-old-self telling her to wait until people will be nice to her. She deserves to operate beyond the truths of who she once was.

You deserve that too.

## ASK QUESTIONS

Despite my inner *Can you* really *do this?* when it came to CrossFit, I kept showing up—pulling away at the rowing machine, learning to climb a rope to the ceiling, and running around the building in the freezing cold—because I was tired of always playing it safe. *Safe keeps us small.* Safe tells us to avoid being a beginner and to keep the equilibrium. Safe told me it was better for me to just run on my neighborhood trail and do workout videos at home (both of which are fine, by the way!). But my spirit wanted more than that. And it was scary to step into a space and pretty much say, "I want to change, I don't know what I'm doing, and I'm here for your support."

My friends, it was beyond just staying safe. Being a beginner and allowing myself to be messy meant learning to ask questions and to trust that no one would care (and that if they did, that wasn't my concern). Over the years, because of the unbalanced caring paradox, I had learned to care way, way, way too much about asking questions or not appearing to have all the answers.

In sixth grade, at my very small Christian day school, I raised my hand one day in religion class because I didn't know what *circumcision* meant. My class had a mix of sixth, seventh, and eighth grades together. We must have been learning about Abraham or some Old Testament ritual that day, and that word wasn't one I knew. My hand was up for most of the class, but my teacher, Mr. Fritze, never called on me.

Fast-forward to years later, when I learned what circumcision is. Do you know what my first thought was? Thank goodness I wasn't called on in class that day! Asking questions can be risky! You ask a "wrong" question and get ridiculed, and you ask good, thought-out questions, and you get praised. You can even ask questions that everyone knows the answers to or questions that make them uncomfortable and then be the butt of jokes.

But sometimes, others judge even your good question or assume you're just trying to be seen. Never mind the saying that all questions are good questions—deep down, we've all experienced the truth that asking questions can be vulnerable.

Even though we're told that asking questions is part of the process of learning, the act itself also means admitting, "I don't understand this thing I'm asking a question about." My false narrative about questions said that asking meant not that I was curious but that I wasn't prepared. In my mind, questions meant a person wasn't as smart—versus looking at it as being smart enough to ask. And questions focused the spotlight on the asker and on what that person didn't know.

The first day of CrossFit, I observed.

The second day of CrossFit, I resolved to ask questions.

If I didn't understand something, I asked questions, even if they might be about basic things. Being willing to ask questions is a good thing, especially if you're lifting heavy things over your head! Not asking would have been riskier than whatever supposed embarrassment might come alongside revealing that I didn't know how to do something. If I had assumed how to get the bar back on the rack instead of learning to rely on my spotter, I could have been injured. Assumptions can be dangerous!

When you give yourself grace to ask questions, you open the doorway to learning. My kids are always asking Siri or Alexa questions. Neither device tells them they're dumb for asking questions; they just answer with information. Your progress will slow down and your potential will be dulled if you assume that not asking the questions is the stronger route to take.

Ask them. Be brave. Learn.

## GET MESSY

Getting messy is part of being a beginner. If you're going to paint your living room, your living room will get messy. You can't start a painting project and expect it to stay pristine. Getting messy is part of life and part of change. One of the reasons we don't get messy is that we live in a judgmental world. If you want to go all in on life, to reignite your spark, you're going to need to deal with your own thoughts about judging and be willing to create a bit of mess in your life. To do this, I believe you have to commit to three important principles:

1.  Don't assume that others are judging you.
2.  Don't judge others.
3.  Stop judging yourself so harshly.

Every single reason I gave Dan on the first day was a derivative of one of these three things. I prejudged the CrossFit crowd. Holy moly, was I wrong. Even though each class is a mix of beginners, mid-levels, and pros, *no one cares* what level you're at. Most people are just happy that you've decided to embark on this adventure! They're *fine* with you not being perfect at each exercise, with you making mistakes, with you needing to ask questions, and they want you to keep trying.

Other class members aren't there to judge the people around them; they're there to push themselves to get better. When someone keeps trying, keeps going after it, it motivates other people to get on the floor, to count out reps for another person, and to scream, "You've got this!"

Most participants are there to be the "You can do this" voice for others.

## Don't Assume Others Are Judging

My first mistake in CrossFit was assuming that everyone was judging me. They're not. They're there to work out, to better themselves, and they choose to do it with a group. If anything, I discovered that most participants find deep value in the culture of everyone pushing each other to succeed. It's not about who's the best (let's face it, I'm not going to outlift a 210-pound man on a bench press) but about each person bettering *their own* best. Beyond that, most are there to push everyone else to better themselves. I didn't realize this when I started and was letting my teenage brain take over and assume everyone would be judging me. The moment we push aside assumptions and allow truth to reveal itself is when we have the power to continue to add fuel to our fire.

No one cared that I didn't know the acronyms AMRAP, WOD, or EMOM. They didn't laugh when I asked. They didn't tell me I wouldn't amount to anything (like those thirteen-year-old bullies did). They didn't shun me because I was last to finish the workout of the day (WOD). They weren't competitors but rather allies, not bullies but friends.

I had forgotten that nearly every person in that class also sat in an office or picked up after kids or labored at some other job and then walked in these doors and stepped on the futuristic scale, took the almost-naked before picture, put money down, and agreed to show up. Most folks at my gym were normal people like you and me who were challenging themselves, not professional athletes. And no one was forced into that gym. Everyone came by choice—even if they had to battle with themselves to get in the door!

## THE POWER OF VULNERABILITY

For me, CrossFit is community. Camaraderie. We're all there for the same thing—to be the best we can be and to cheer along our comrades.

It is essential to find a group of people who will let you be the beginner without judgment. If you join a group and it's not that, you can leave (you're not thirteen anymore—you can choose what's right for you). If anyone cares about your outfit at CrossFit, it's probably not the right gym. If they care about your shoes because they don't have enough support, those are your people. Your community should be exactly that—your community. A good community will encourage you, celebrate your wins with you, and expect you to do the same for them.

You need to give yourself time to create these friendships and bonds. It's unreasonable to expect day one, week one, or even month one to be full of powerful community moments. Give others a chance and keep showing up. Creating a culture of community takes time.

You have the power to put yourself in powerful situations.

## Don't Judge Others

This also means *I* don't get to be judgy either. What if I had walked into CrossFit and immediately started judging others—but then expected that no one would judge me? First, there's simply not enough time to be judging others (or comparing, which I guess is the "nicer" way to describe it). The time you spend judging another person is time you could spend bettering yourself or learning about their story. Judging is the presupposition that you know the inner chapters of their story based on a very external glimpse. Second, judging can lead to gossiping, which is so harmful and creates a negative and hurtful dynamic that also harms you in the process (and it can take you right back to some of those times in life when you were the one being gossiped about). Third, judging holds *everyone* back. It harms the person being judged, and it harms the one doing the judging too. It's like a hangnail—it's annoying and painful, and even though it's small, it needs to be cut off.

The easiest way to stay small and to keep your ember just barely flickering is to judge those around you. It's hard to spark that ember to a flame if you're focused on judging others. People can sense it. And it's harming your internal life whether you realize it or not.

Don't be that person. Cut off judging.

### Stop Judging Yourself So Harshly

Finally, when you judge yourself harshly, oftentimes with a measuring stick much stricter than you'd use for anyone else, it's time to stop. Remind your inner critic that its job is to be the adviser and also your advocate. It's one thing to hold the bar for yourself high and another to hold it so high that you preemptively cut yourself down.

Holding the bar means expecting great things of yourself but also being okay with imperfection. Cutting yourself down means telling yourself you're an idiot because you couldn't figure it out and offering no grace or compassion.

Listen to the words you use to describe yourself. Would you use those same words to talk to your friends? Your kids? Your spouse? If not, stop using them to describe yourself. You aren't a loser because your painting at the Paint and Sip class doesn't look like the teacher's (or the dude's sitting next to you). You joined the class and you're learning. That's what matters. You aren't a failure if you can't run a 5K in under thirty minutes. No one said there had to be a time limit. You're running! You're exercising and pushing yourself. You are taking care of your body. You aren't dumb if you end up in last place at trivia night. You are at trivia night—for fun! You are trying. You are doing something other than your normal. You are doing it!

Be inspired by others. Be their cheerleader.

*And be your own cheerleader as well.*

◄ ✦ ►

Remember, your only bar of comparison in examining yourself is yourself—the you of today versus the you of the past. You are the only thing to compare yourself against! It doesn't matter what your neighbor is doing, what big thing is going on in a coworker's life, or how social media might make you think your life should be going.

Are *you* improving?

Are *you* happier?

Are *you* adding value?

Are *you* taking care of yourself?

That's the comparison.

My CrossFit app only lists my progress. It doesn't show the progress of the person across the gym. As I watched my pace and progress with each class, I started to realize that improving wasn't about being better than someone else—it was about being better *than me* when I began. My experience in CrossFit was a real-life green-shorts moment. I had never done dead lifts, power cleans, power jerks, or any kind of exercise with me lifting a bar with giant weights. But I had tossed aside those green shorts that no longer fit what I wanted to pursue and was in that gym, learning, trying, and consistently getting better.

*Responsibility and taking chances aren't always dependent on each other. Sure, if you sell everything, pack your kids up, and move to Mongolia, then perhaps they are. But even a big change like this is a chance, and perhaps you would be giving your kids the greatest childhood ever. Somewhere around fifteen is when we start being asked, "What do you want to do with your life?" and then at about thirty the phrase shifts from "What do you want to do?" to "You better have it figured out by now." We need some pressure to figure things out. I love my kids, but I don't want them living at home when they're forty because they're still figuring it out.*

*You can be responsible and take chances.*

*They're not mutually exclusive.*

Are you fearful because whatever you're interested in—going after that promotion, finally letting yourself dream again, buying that house, starting the nonprofit, figuring out you again, and so on—scares you? Are you afraid of failing or of not knowing how to start? That fear means whatever it is you are interested in *matters* to you. If you didn't have emotion tied to it, it wouldn't be that big of a deal to you.

Be grateful for the fear, and don't let it stop you. Let it motivate you! Let it motivate you to make these next chapters in your life full of starting new things—and continuing them. Be proud of being a beginner. It means you aren't sitting on the sidelines of your life.

The only thing harder than being a beginner is *never* being a beginner. And when you're never the beginner, fear will be replaced by regret. You don't want to regret not taking the chances, making the mistakes, or getting messy. This is your shot, your chance to try.

One last thing about lifting heavy things, about taking chances: if you want to experience change, you must put it on your to-do list that *today* you are lifting heavy things. You're not *going* to do it. You *are doing* it. You've got to have it as part of the plan. If you want to change the future, you must make a solid plan to change today. Otherwise you won't ever do it. Make the plan. Do it.

You can lift heavy things. I promise you.

## FIRE STARTERS

✦ **Create an offensive versus defensive strategy.** If you sign up for an art class, ask if there are other beginners in the class. Ask if the class is open to questions. And pay attention to what you sign up for. If you've never painted and sign up for an advanced "Paint Like Monet" class, you're making it harder on yourself. Be willing to go up the ladder of learning instead of trying to skip rungs. In swimming lessons when I was a kid, there was a kid in the class who was much older. That didn't stop him. He kept showing up, kept diving, kept practicing the crawl stroke. Sometimes you have to put yourself in the class that fits you, not where you wish you could be. The process of learning is what makes the experience amazing. You are worth not shortchanging your process.

✦ **Practice being the beginner.** If you really love to crochet, teach others how to do it. When you teach others, you learn how to be a beginner. You'll develop empathy for those starting (and will be proud of their success), and you'll also develop a higher level of empathy for yourself when the roles are reversed. And don't just stay in what you know! Take more advanced classes for yourself. You might discover other facets of whatever that pursuit is that you truly love.

✦ **Be willing to document your before.** How many super inspiring stories start with a before image? Whether it's a health journey, a financial journey, or even a remodel, the before image holds so much power because it illustrates what happens when a beginner puts in the work. Every single person who says yes to a before picture more intentionally pursues having an after photo. I'm grateful for those CrossFit pictures. I'm also grateful for the pictures of the projects we've taken on in our home. I'm grateful for the pictures my oldest, Han, took during the hard single-mom days of my life. They documented a raw me but a brave me, and I'm unbelievably grateful for those images. Make an effort to record yourself when you embark on your soul-spark journey. I can guarantee you that you will be proud to look back at that picture. And more than anything, you will be grateful you tried.

# CHAPTER 8

# IS IT EVEN POSSIBLE?

## How Effort and Consistency Can Make the Impossible Possible

Twenty minutes from my parents' home in Minnesota stood an icon of my preteen and teenage existence—Ridgedale Mall. This mall was your classic mid-eighties design: four flagship stores surrounding a central courtyard with multiple fountains, benches, and kiosks full of perfume samples, rock band T-shirts, and neon trinkets. Near one of the four entrances was the arcade, that dark, teenage-smelling room full of blinking lights, Pac-Man, Space Invaders, pinball, and a row of claw machines.

Ah, the claw machine, the ultimate money suck, the game of eternal hope. Once, when I was twelve or so, on one of the first times my parents let me be there without them (they'd be picking me up at eight outside the Applebee's entrance), I wasted all my money on the claw machine in an attempt to retrieve some musty, neon-colored stuffed animal. My preteen brain was determined to make it work, believed I'd be different from all the other losers, and assumed I'd ultimately be victorious. I'd line the claw up, push the button, watch the metal jaws drop and clip a corner of the stuffed animal—only to then watch it slip out of the jaws and back into the pile.

When the quarters were gone that night, I remember feeling embarrassed. How had I lost my money playing such a stupid, pointless game? I had nothing to show for my empty wallet except a busted ego and a bunch of friends who watched my money slip away. On the car ride home, after some "I'm fine's" and moping, my dad asked if I had fun.

I told him I lost all my money on that game.

As I braced for the lecture on the wise use of money, my dad instead asked me again if I had fun. Fun? It was fun in the moment for sure, but now, afterward, I had nothing tangible to hold to prove the fun. And then instead of a rebuke, my dad simply told me it's never about the stuffed animal but rather the experience.

I could have lost my babysitting money playing Space Invaders or spent it on the teeniest dish of pink bubblegum ice cream at Baskin Robbins or on a clearance shirt from the back corner of The Gap. Instead, that night, I chose to play a game.

I put my money, my time, and my energy into the thrill of the potential.

## THE POWER OF EFFORT

In spring 2024, we took our kids to Branson, Missouri, for spring break. Normally, we trek south to the Gulf of Mexico (like the Navarre Beach trip), but this year we ventured west to the land of after-dinner shows and theme parks. The VRBO we found in Branson was part of a giant resort complex and had a game room with pool tables, video games, and, you guessed it, multiple claw machines. It felt like a full-circle moment with that eighties arcade.

Instead of a pocketful of quarters, we loaded up game cards for the kids to scan before playing games. At one point, I saw my bonus daughter (my stepdaughter, but *bonus* is so much nicer), Millie, in the room with a ridiculous number of claw machines. The adult in me wanted to tell her it's impossible to win—until I remembered that it's not about winning. It's about the experience, the trying again, the adjusting, the thrill of it all.

We had made a choice to give the money to spend to have fun. It wasn't my choice whether it should be spent on Skee-Ball or basketball or the claw machine. This was Millie's moment, just like it was mine thirty-five years prior.

I watched her. Cheered her on. And reminded myself, again, that the easiest way to douse someone's excitement is to tell them it's impossible before they even try.

If you're like me, you've got a pretty extensive tally sheet of all the people and experiences that have told or showed you why it's better to stay safe on the sidelines and not even try. I don't believe most of us set out to snuff out the sparks of those around us (or ourselves). Yet we live in a world where we're often told that dreams are impractical—at least for us. We need to get the stable job first—then we can find time to "safely" go after our dreams. So we keep pushing the dream aside.

Perhaps you were told in a creative writing class (which you loved) that you weren't creative and inventive enough. You believed those words and don't allow yourself to pursue it. Or maybe you tried to become the president of the PTO but you didn't get the votes because you were the new mom. Instead of making friends, you decided that if it didn't happen, it would never happen, so you never run again and avoid going to the meetings. Or maybe you sign up for a triathlon, train, and everyone immediately passes you in the swimming portion. You catch your breath, and during the bike portion, you decide you're not cut out for this experience. So the next day you list your bike on Marketplace and determine that you should only compete in running races. These experiences, like a regulator on a car, keep us going a certain speed—fast enough but no faster. (In case you don't know, a regulator sets the vehicle's speed. Most rental trucks have this and won't let the driver go above seventy miles per hour. Trust me, I know.) They decide, "This is your max potential."

Regulators in life eliminate possibilities because they limit potential. The regulators in our lives—whether imposed on us or something we place on ourselves—keep us at a steady pace and don't allow deviation. For so much of my life, I lived with regulators that I thought were impossible to remove—regulators on my time, on my level of freedom, on the parameters of discomfort I could tolerate. And the limits I placed on myself by believing that were profound.

The "impossible" claw machine? It is in fact possible— if you try.

It *is* possible to figure it out, to make adjustments, lift the same prize over and over until it fits perfectly in the claw and is dropped into the chute and into your hands. Yes, there's an expense—money and time—and it's fraught with challenges, but it is still possible. At some point, many of us have decided that the time and money needed to win the prize isn't worth it. So we don't try at all, or we quit. Or we believe others will think we're foolish for going after something they might think pointless. Sometimes it's us telling everyone else, "Don't bother. It's a waste of time."

But if you keep at it, learn from your mistakes, you will eventually win and walk away with a prize and the evidence of your effort. You can learn pretty quickly which kids have gotten good at the claw game because they know which toys you can win and which are stuck in the machine for life. They have put in the time and broken down the process of how to win. But at one point, they, too, were claw machine rookies.

The only way to accomplish things is to try.

If you want to really find yourself and find your spark, you must be willing to look at the beliefs you've put on your life and work to remove them if they don't serve you anymore. We are the ultimate cheerleaders for our kids: "Just try, guys! You can do it!" But then we turn around and speak unkindly to ourselves: "There's no point. You can't do it anyway."

*Running has been a huge part of my soul's self-discovery. It's just me, my thoughts, and the trail. I've spent hours and hours reflecting and listening to my soul and the regulators I've put on my story—one of them being, "You should be done running now. You're tired." Instead of sinking into and accepting that it's impossible for me to run farther, there are many days, even today, when instead of focusing on the end goal, I tell myself to just run to the crosswalk, then to the stop sign, then to the lake, then to the turnaround. The motto "Just Try" has helped me finish many things.*

The "10,000-Hour rule," which Malcolm Gladwell covers in his book *Outliers*, presents the theory that you can master pretty much anything with consistent practice—to the tune of, yep, 10,000 hours. Gladwell doesn't mince words, doesn't say it will be easy, but instead demonstrates how consistent effort *will* produce results.[11]

I've played piano since I was five. Because of more than forty years sitting on a wooden bench in front of various pianos, I can open up my book of Mozart and pretty much play any piece. I've practiced for so many hours and have gotten to the point where I don't worry if I can play a song because *I know I can*. The effect of effort allows us to move from wondering if we can accomplish something to knowing it is within our scope of capabilities.

The reason I can read sheet music is because I put in the effort—learning and failing and practicing and learning some more. It meant many weeks, months, and years of playing the wrong notes, the wrong rhythm, the wrong tempo, and with the wrong phrasing. Eventually, through belief and practice, you begin to play the right notes, your fingers catch up to your brain, you feel the beat, and more than that, you develop the ability to anticipate the next note. The committed practice begins to produce the desired end result.

Michael Jordan didn't become one of the greatest basketball players in history because he didn't miss shots. He missed more critical shots than he made.[12] When you miss the shot, play the wrong note, say the wrong thing, drop the claw at the wrong time, you are learning what not to do so you can make adjustments to do what you need to do.

Every single stumble allows our brains to make a correction for next time if we give ourselves patience and grace and have the stick-to-it-ive-ness to keep trying. So often, instead of trying again, we allow the missteps, the newness, the failures to tell us, "You tried, you failed, that's enough." Or we tell ourselves, "It was dumb to even try this. It's too hard. Why on earth do you think you'd be good at this? Save your time and money. Don't make a fool out of yourself."

My piano teacher never told me to stop because I played the wrong note. She'd simply say, "Start again." My parents endured years of listening to me hit wrong notes. They sat through recitals on uncomfortable church pews, listening to kid after kid whose parents had decided to put money into them learning an art. Instead of letting me goof around, which is what I wanted to do, they dealt with a cranky kid on a Saturday afternoon who had several days of practicing to make up. They had to be willing to let me make a fool out of myself. They knew if I didn't put in the effort, I'd be the kid at the recital who forgot her music. They kept taking me to lessons, even if it meant it was uncomfortable for them. They kept pushing, because they knew that results and discipline only happened with consistent effort. Maybe I would have been terrible at piano, maybe all the notes I memorized would have been forgotten, maybe I would have cried onstage, but none of those maybes mattered—what mattered was that they believed I could push through the slog of learning and succeed.

They could have saved their money, decided that learning piano didn't have purpose and that I might never hit the right notes. But instead, they persisted. They persisted because they could see the greater vision, what could be, what I would ultimately learn, versus the moments of plunking scales and trying to get my hands to play together.

And the power of that effort paid off—because all these years later, that skill still lives in me and I can call on it at any time. And in fact, playing the piano is another place where my soul comes alive. My parents gave me an amazing gift by insisting that I kept going.

That is what happens when you push through and keep practicing. Practicing also cultivates happiness. The more you work to get your spark back, the more you practice, and the more you practice, the happier you will become. This happiness is a result of the pride in the effort you are giving.

## PRACTICE MAKES PROGRESS

As an adult, when people found out I played piano, they would ask me to teach their kids. For a couple years, I drove to various houses, sat next to kids who wanted to play ragtime but were instead learning how to keep a beat and play scales. I'd work with these kids on reading music and having proper form. The goal wasn't just to get them reading music; it was to ignite a spark of appreciation for music in them.

At one point, I was teaching two neighbor kids who were the same age in back-to-back lessons. Since they were both new, they started at the same spot, in the *Piano Adventures* primer book by Faber and Faber.[13] My goal was twofold: teach them how to read music *and* make appreciating music part of their lives.

Despite both boys starting on page one on the same day, as the months passed, their ease in moving to the next lesson diverged. One of the boys started to pull ahead of his friend. I found myself not having to reteach concepts or reassign lessons to him. For a bit, I tried to keep them together—to act as the regulator that kept both boys on the same trajectory and speed—but then I realized I was holding the second boy back. I realized I needed to talk to the moms who had hired me and figure out how to tactfully explain what was happening. Up until that point, if Kid A was playing "Alouette," Kid B was as well.

One afternoon, after lessons, I chatted with the moms and asked how they thought it was going. As we talked, it became clear why the two boys were advancing at different rates: one mom would sit with her son while he practiced, ensuring that he worked through all the steps and put in the needed practice time. The other mom didn't enforce practice time and just wanted him to have fun. She didn't listen to his practice, didn't suggest corrections—she simply let him do what he wanted to do. Both parents had equally valid strategies. But because they had different strategies, they couldn't expect the same result. And my approach to teaching them changed once I realized they were on different trajectories.

Once you decide to try something new, once you've moved from impossible to possible, don't forget that the amount of effort you put in *will* affect the outcome. Consistent effort isn't perfection, and it isn't always fun, but the willingness to invest time and effort with the belief that you will get better can have huge results in so many areas. The irony for me as the teacher was that I felt at the beginning that Kid A had natural talent—but he didn't progress as quickly because he wasn't practicing. Just because you're naturally good at something doesn't mean you don't have to work at it.

But you also don't have to come up with ten thousand hours to learn something new. Bestselling author of *The First 20 Hours*, Josh Kaufman, shares how you can learn anything and be pretty good at it if you put in twenty hours of committed practice.[14] To prove the theory, he decided to learn a song on the ukulele, which he'd never played, before a giant TedX keynote. He discovered he needed to know only four chords, and then he committed to practicing twenty minutes a day for thirty days and performed the song live onstage.[15] And he was good!

Even with or without natural talent, progress requires consistent effort and dedication.

Let's go back to Michael Jordan. Clearly, he entered the court with some inherent talent. He could have decided that he was so talented he didn't need to practice. He also could have decided, after missing some free throws, that maybe he wasn't cut out for basketball after all. Neither of these decisions would have led to the world of Air Jordans and Chicago Bulls championships.

Living with fire, with your spark ignited, requires committed effort coupled with the belief that your effort will produce results. Success isn't dependent on never falling. Success includes falling so we learn how to stand up again and again and persist.

Commitment—in other words, *practice*—will help you maintain your internal flame.

In 2022, I ran a thousand miles. People have asked how I was able to do that. I tell them it wasn't ever about the thousand miles; it was about the three miles in front of me every day. I had to accept that the impossible could be made possible three miles at a time.

Society tries to convince us that we can make a change in six weeks with four easy steps every day for fifteen minutes. But what happens after six weeks? What happens on week six, day one, when the program is over? The best athletes, performers, writers, creators, gardeners, and bakers realize that true success isn't a program—it's a lifestyle of doing. Josh Kaufman could only play the one song on the uke. If he wanted to get better, he would need to commit to another twenty hours, and then another. The reason his speech is so powerful is that it illuminates the power in consistent, small efforts, and often that effort is the catalyst that reignites the spark of possibility.

What are you doing right now? What in your life would fit in the category of "This is for me"? A lot of people will tell me that running isn't their thing. That's great! Maybe they'll like walking instead. If they don't like walking, I encourage them to try swimming, painting, singing, learning an instrument, rock climbing, playing pickleball. The choices for leisure activities are abundant. If you can't think of where to invest your time, go back a couple chapters and go through the list of fifty questions again. And think back to your childhood . . . maybe you learned to play piano, like me. Have you thought of sitting down and playing? Look at the list of your message markers, too, to find your "this is for me" place to start.

This applies to your big, bold, audacious, risky-feeling dreams and passion projects as well. If you have the dream to advance in your career, what small steps can you take now to move the needle forward? If you want to create your nonprofit, are there others you could shadow so you can learn? If you want to go back to school and get your degree, what is the first step? Your dream is out there waiting for you to embrace it . . . and to start practicing. Put in the practice, one step, one mile, one phone call, one day at a time.

## POSSIBILITIES, NOT IMPROBABILITIES

I want you to see the possibilities versus the improbabilities in life.

About six years ago, my daughter Grace, who was seventeen at the time, won a fishing lure out of a claw machine at Reeds Bait in northern Minnesota. Whoever came up with the idea to stock a claw machine with boxed fishing lures and pop it right in the middle of the busiest bait shop in town should get a bonus. The machine always had a line, and a crowd watched as adults maneuvered the claw into the pile below. The adults would cheer each other on, and whenever a winning lure dropped into the chute, a loud collective cheer would fill the room. The day

Grace won, she stood in the middle of the crowd while her siblings peered through the glass, cheering her on. She had already spent more than the price of the lure, but she didn't care. She wanted to be the one to win the lure out of that machine. Finally, on attempt fifteen or so, she wrapped the claw around the rectangular box, maneuvered it to the chute, and dropped it in as a collective cheer filled the room.

Grace now lives near Washington, DC, with her husband, Miguel. A couple summers ago, our family's summer vacation was to DC, Philly, Baltimore, and, of course, to visit Grace and Miguel. A couple days before we left Nashville, I climbed into our attic and pulled down the plastic boxes labeled "Grace." She had carefully packed them before leaving for basic training. It had been bittersweet to watch her go through all her earthly possessions, deciding what to donate, toss, or keep.

Up in the scorching heat of the attic, in one of those boxes I would be toting to DC, was the lure she won from the claw machine. *She had kept it.* As I was writing this chapter, my curiosity was piqued, and I texted Grace to ask if she still had that lure.

"Yes, of course," she said, as if I would have even questioned it.

I realized in that moment that the lure mattered to her. She didn't keep it because it's valuable or an heirloom of some kind (heck, not only is that lure the most expensive lure she owns; it's the *only* lure she owns). She's not saving it to go fishing someday. She saved it because it means something to her. That lure symbolized the impossible made possible. She once told me she knew she could get that lure if she just let herself figure out the strategy—and then followed through until the strategy worked. The lure was never about fishing; it was about proving something to herself. This spring, I once again visited her, and sitting proudly, front and center, out on the shelf in her living room is that lure.

Fact: we don't lose the hope, the possibility, of winning, just like we don't lose our ember.

What's the impossible-possible lure in your life? Start looking around you for items in your life that symbolize something that seemed impossible . . . but ended up being possible. Maybe it's the diploma you stored away but was so powerful when you accepted it. Or your ultrasound picture after a long infertility journey. Or maybe it's the picture of you signing the mortgage papers of your first home. And if you can't find one of these items yet (you will in the future), go to Walmart, buy a lure, and let it be your reminder of what is possible. Put it somewhere you'll see it often, and let yourself dream—and then *act*—on whatever it is that stirs the flames of your heart.

You can make the impossible possible. Continue to let yourself try.

## FIRE STARTERS

✦ **Find a physical symbol for the impossibilities becoming possible.** The universe is exceptionally equipped to help you find one as well. Before I started writing this book, images of turtles (and *actual* turtles) kept showing up in my life. I ordered a surprise gift from a specialty company at Christmas, and twice it was a stone turtle (maybe they had an abundance, but they were different turtles). My mother-in-law brought me back a bracelet from a trip—surprise!—turtles. My friend Catherine began seeing turtles and would send pictures. My husband rescued a turtle from the street and put it in our backyard by the creek. My son Elijah drew a turtle on a card for me. Turtles were everywhere. I finally realized turtles were a symbol for the writing process. It's never fast—slow and steady wins the race. Sitting next to my MacBook most days is one of those stone turtles, reminding me to plod on.

+ **Try Kaufman's twenty-hour challenge.** This will require blocking off those hours and putting in consistent effort and practice. Don't quit on hour two, ten, or nineteen—continue to push through. And then share your result! Write about it, post about it on social, share it with me. When you share, you will inspire another person to try something new. The reason short challenges help is that they are a boost to your spark. Once the spark is lit, continue the momentum and keep fueling it.

# CHAPTER 9

# WHAT IF I DON'T HAVE TIME?

## *It's Never Too Late to Set an Audacious Goal*

My running story has perhaps the least glamorous start. I never took those first steps with the intention of doing anything spectacular. The first time I went was only because Dan asked me if I'd run with him. I was huffing and puffing that first time and questioning the sanity of runners (and myself for saying yes!). But I kept going, kept lacing up my shoes, kept getting out there. Eventually, I started running races and setting goals. But that first day? I just ran.

I also quit.

Most of the time, I didn't *plan* to quit—it just happened. It's not like there was a date on my calendar that said, "Today is your last day of running for a really, really, really long time. Enjoy!" Rather, it was a day off that led to another day off that led to another day off that led to, well, you get it. Quitting.

Starting up again after quitting isn't easy. It's downright hard. There's the inner monologue of "you quit again" and the physical load of "I can't breathe and my legs are like lead." Once I have quit, part of me doesn't want to deal with the reality of starting over. *Again.* So I do the next best thing—I wait. Which turns out to be the worst thing! Because now I'm making starting up again even harder. I hate quitting. But I hate even more the parts of me that are *willing* to quit in the first place.

But is it considered quitting if I start up again? What constitutes *actually* quitting and isn't just a pause? I'd mull over these questions on my runs and in my writing, trying to find answers. While I celebrated some places in life where quitting was beneficial—I had quit staying small, had quit staying silent, had quit holding on to things— some of the areas I was quitting weren't helping me. And I began to realize—quitting hard but necessary things meant I might be compromising on myself.

If I was going to live above the radar—something I was so committed to in so many areas of my life—I needed to determine what allowed me to give myself a pass when I shouldn't be taking it in the first place. I decided that taking a rest day so my muscles could heal wasn't a pass, but deciding I just didn't feel like running was a pass. That "I just don't feel like it" became my litmus test.

I discovered that this scenario was true in so many other areas of my life. There is so much stuff I don't feel like doing that still needs to be done. I didn't feel like dealing with creditors years ago, but it still needed to be done. I don't feel like cleaning the bathrooms, but come on now, that *definitely* needs to be done. I don't feel like doing edits, but even those edits need to be done (if they aren't, you wouldn't be reading these words!). Compromise allows us to rationalize the feeling of deserving a break or being too tired. And I had grown sick of my own quick ability to compromise.

The antidote? I changed how I described myself. Instead of describing what I wanted to do, I stated who I would *be* by doing that action. Instead of "I'm going for a run," I would say, "I am a runner." Rather than "I'm going to write a book," it became "I am an author." Instead of "I'm going to take care of my health," I would say, "I am healthy." That simple reframe helped me realize that I needed to remove the word *going* from my to-do list and I needed to *be* the thing I was striving for.

> I am running today.
> I am writing today.
> I am speaking up today.
> I am paying the bills today.
> I am meeting with a friend today.
> I am investing in my story today.

What might this list look like for you? Are there things in your life that you consistently allow yourself a pass on or that you quit again and again? Try to catch yourself using the words "going to" related to some task ("I'm going to make that doctor appointment," "I'm going to take a walk after dinner"). Then ask yourself why you haven't done it yet, and make a goal to get it done. "Going to" is the language of someday. Notice I ended each of my "I am" statements with *today*. You still might feel uneasy trying to define who you want to be, or you might feel you're not qualified to carry that title, but it's critical to begin living out who you want to become. If the person you envision yourself to be walks confidently into a boardroom and leads the meeting, that's your example. If the person you want to become composes music, you need to start defining yourself as a composer. If the person you want to be has her spark back, you need to start defining yourself as the girl on fire. Unstoppable.

## SET THE AUDACIOUS GOAL

Even though I had quit so many times, I started running. Again. This time, however, beyond reframing the task and how I defined myself, I added two more things: goals and accountability. I also challenged my own presupposition that the only way I could finish something was if *someone else* was holding my feet to the fire. Someone holding your feet to the fire goes a step beyond accountability or a check-in. It's the drill sergeant screaming at Grace to keep going when she wanted to quit. And there's a place for that (but not at boot camp). Sometimes we need another person screaming at us not to give up when every cell wants to fold. But that isn't accountability. It's something more—it's reliance on someone else to keep you moving or motivated. If you need someone else, especially in the beginning, you can find another person to hold you accountable. That is you taking accountability.

Instead of believing I needed someone else to keep me on track, I wanted the motivator to be *me*. I wanted to figure out how to push through my own mental drama and finish something because I had the inner fortitude. I had done some really big things—walking into an attorney's office, signing papers, moving across the country—but I didn't know how to create that urgency in other spaces in my life. Back then, I was still the queen of procrastination, of slick reasons to wait and other tasks to accomplish. Why couldn't I do what really mattered to me?

In 2022, I set an audacious running goal with the hopes that I'd overcome my compromising tendencies in the process. The goal had poignancy because the distance was the mileage, 899 miles, between my Nashville home and my parents' Minneapolis home. Part of me needed to prove to myself that if the world went sideways (the pandemic sure taught me it could), I could run/walk to my parents' home if I needed to. This goal gave me the chance to practice that first step of debunking the impossible. This was a chance to flip that belief on its head. While it would take me a *long* time to trek this distance, I knew it was possible.

*Goal setting is tricky. We tend to both set goals beyond our scope of self and also set goals that are far too low. When you're looking at your goals, it's probably not realistic to put down "Swim around Key West" when you don't know how to swim. (This is an actual race my husband wants to do. He wants me on the boat to help reapply sunscreen and be on shark lookout duty.) The better starting goal? "Start swimming two laps a day at the YMCA." Then, when you complete that goal, make a newer, bigger one. Goal setting is leap-frogging up.*

But then came the question: If I believed this goal was possible, what was the stall?

In January, I started running. Then I got sick and stopped running. After I was better, and because it was early enough in the year for the goal to still be possible, I started running again. And I kept running. I ran by moms and dads pushing strollers, older couples, people with dogs (I always get way on the other side), and friends as I racked up the miles, clocking in at just under one hundred miles most months. My favorite element of running is that it gives me time, a great deal of time, to think. And during all those minutes and hours, I discovered why I have compromised and stalled so much in the past: I was afraid of commitment.

I hate breaking commitments. It makes me feel like a loser or a failure. So instead of breaking them, I often compromise and never even make the commitments in the first place.

Deadlines have stressed me out since I first learned what a deadline was. I had always assumed that the pressure of the deadline itself was the stressor. What I didn't understand is that underneath the pressure are those pesky lies of "What if I fail?" and "What if I let someone down?" Because I had begun working through some of these narratives and beliefs in counseling, those lies fell flat. I knew that the only person I'd be letting down by not following through on my running goal was me.

My husband, kids, neighbors, readers, family, and whoever else would survive if I didn't keep my commitment. I was the one who would be let down if I gave up, and because of that fear, I was terrified to commit. I didn't want to disappoint myself again.

Disappointing ourselves is an often unspoken-about part of life. It's easier to deal with not wanting to disappoint others, partially because of the external pressure to keep up with the Joneses. Disappointing ourselves, though, is another matter. It's a painful shadow story many of us have had to deal with, and it can bring with it shame that we dropped the ball on our own story. Again. One of the best ways to stop letting yourself down is to ask yourself if you'd respond to a friend in the same way you respond to yourself. Would you encourage her to keep trying, even in the hard? Would you help her figure it out, even if she didn't have answers? Would you tell her you believe in her, even if she doubts? Chances are great that you would. Be the friend to yourself that you would be to others.

As I worked through all of this on the trail one day, tears ran down my face. I realized I didn't love my own story the way I loved everyone else's story. I wouldn't allow myself to forget my failures and so often used those failures to define my potential. My safeguard? I thought I was safe if I sat on the sidelines with a small, doable goal.

In counseling years ago, I learned a way to deal with the parts of our thinking that still have a grip on our present moment. The fear of commitment and disappointing myself was deep-rooted. The years of financial ruin and not finishing college chipped away at my ego. I was embarrassed by my own story and had developed a part of my thinking that would play it safe and oftentimes quit before she started. The technique I learned to break out of this was to thank the mode of thinking that keeps us safe and then to simply say, "I'm no longer there in that moment. I need you to become confident [or whatever you need or want now] and rise to the new me."

Sometimes we live with the strategies of our earlier selves. It's like those green shorts all over again, but in this case, the limitation is on our capabilities. Our thought processes are fast, sometimes instantaneous, and unless we challenge those thoughts with one of this book's theme questions—"Why do you think that to be true?"—an old thought pattern that is no longer useful can influence a now decision. If you want to change, you first must identify the previous line of thinking, be grateful for it (chances are, that line of thinking protected you), and then replace it with something new that rises to where you are now.

Releasing the old thought opens up room for the new thoughts; the old strategies can be replaced by new. Releasing an old thought involves four things:

1. **Be grateful for the old pattern.** Remember, the you from years ago, who adopted the initial pattern, probably did the best she should. Give her credit.

2. **Learn from the pattern.** Ask yourself, *What is the purpose of this pattern?* It might be to protect you or to keep you safe. Most of our thinking boils down to keeping us safe, feeling loved, and knowing we are worthy. Once you know why the pattern is there, be grateful again for the information your mind has given you.

3. **Create a new pattern.** If you need to speak up but the fear of others stops you, a new pattern

WHAT IF I DON'T HAVE TIME?

would be, "I am confident onstage and the words come naturally to me." Creating a new pattern requires you to reframe the old pattern with a new, positive, and empowering result.

4. **Repeat the new pattern.** Practice telling yourself the new pattern and catch yourself if you slip into the old. This is classic visualization—seeing the future you in the present and stepping into that truth. Write the new pattern down, and give yourself permission to believe it.

The thanking portion might seem strange, but it's powerful and important. The you from years ago more than likely made the best decisions within her power at the time. You need to forgive yourself for the mistakes, thank yourself for what you did to survive, and love yourself enough to move on. If we don't learn to extend gratitude to our old thinking for how it got us to where we are now, it's like being in a leaking boat and not trying to repair it. Maybe you patch it temporarily, but the leak will continue. You need to do more than patch it—you must accept that there is a leak and then fully repair it.

Repairing it for me? It involved thanking my younger self for doing her best and then committing to move forward, telling myself that I am capable of big and great things. Every single time I ran, I would tell myself, "I am capable of running 899 miles." Every single time I spoke in front of people I would tell myself, "I am a confident and inspiring speaker."

You are capable of so much too! At the top of your list? You are capable of not quitting on yourself. You are capable of audacious goals. You are capable of being a beginner. You are capable at loving your old story . . . and also of writing a new one. You are capable of reframing your beliefs. You are capable of doing hard things. You are capable of reigniting your life.

## SET YOURSELF UP FOR A STREAK

Toward the end of January, as I sunk into the truth of my capabilities, I pondered ways to keep myself on track. I knew the unpredictability of life, the awaiting speed bumps, so as I ran, I developed a strategy to help me get back on track if and when I fell off track. Notice the *when*. My strategy wasn't to be perfect or to never miss a day—it was simply to keep running while knowing a day would probably come that would knock me off track. If you never allow yourself the space to stumble, you might as well not start. Stumbles happen. The power is in starting up again. The power is also in strategizing for the off-track moments and having a plan in place to help you start again.

When perfectionism creeps into goal setting, it can lead to overwhelm. Overwhelm tells you that there's too much on your plate or that it will be impossible to get back on track. The solution? You need an "overwhelm buster" that says, "I may stumble, but this is how I'm going to get back on track." I used these five steps to get back and stay on track:

1. **Make a chart.** It wasn't anything fancy, just a hand-drawn chart in my notebook with a bunch of squares, each representing two miles. After every run, I'd open the book and color in another square. Yes, it's technically a reward chart, but for me it worked. Not only did I break down how many miles I needed to run each day, but I was able to see my progress at a glance, and by seeing it, I became accountable for the progress. I didn't want to get to the end of the year and come across the page filled in only halfway.

2. **Share your goal.** I posted what I was planning to do on Facebook. On February 1, I posted an image of how far I had run on a map. I explained my goal of running the distance from my home

to my mom and dad's and shared my mileage for the month of January and my insights thus far. My Facebook friends loved this goal. The level of interest and cheering surprised me—and it motivated me to keep going. There were times when I felt like quitting, but I didn't want the next month to go by without posting and everyone saying, "Hey . . . are you still doing this?" I kept sharing for the entire year.

3. **Do the thing.** This might seem obvious, but the only way to stay on track is to do whatever you've set out to do. To accomplish my goal, I had to actually run. If I got behind, the number of miles I had to do the next day would increase. The pressure of that kept me running. I find it helps to also reverse-engineer what you're doing. I knew I needed to run 3.2 miles a day to cover the distance to my parents' home. Knowing that daily math kept me running. If I hadn't taken the time to break it down, each day's goal would have been nebulous. Find the nebulous spots in your goals, and work to make them concrete, measurable, and doable.

4. **Visualize the end result.** I pictured myself running in my parents' neighborhood and into

their driveway. Many days, this visualization kept my feet moving, even if they were slow. Visualization is incredibly powerful because it allows you to see the future you, even with the confines of the current you in place. The me running in March needed to see the me running in October—and to realize just how much the October me was grateful that March me didn't give up.

5. **Learn to say no.** And be confident in your no. My commitment would break down because I'd start to waffle, to people-please at the expense of my own self. I'd feel guilt over the dishes or want to show up for an early-morning coffee with friends. Instead of my answer being a hard no, I learned to say no to the initial invite and yes to the reschedule. It didn't mean I didn't get coffee; it simply meant I didn't during running time. Every single *no* is a *yes* to something else. No isn't selfish either, especially if the no establishes a boundary that allows you to thrive. I also had to say no to my own tendencies to stop. On many days I wanted to quit my run, and I would ask myself, *Why do you want to stop?* When that day's "because" would come out of my mouth, I could pretty quickly see

that I didn't have a compelling reason to listen to my own arguments for stopping. I said no to stopping, which became yes to continuing.

As the days progressed, something powerful emerged—a streak, a progression of days in a row. The longer the streak, the harder it is to break. This year, as I was writing this book, I decided to see how many days in a row I could run. I started January 1. I ran in the snow, ran my cul-de-sac sixty times in a row, ran races, ran when I didn't want to . . . I just kept running.

And I ended up running seventy-five days in a row.

Dan's friend Bert golfs on January 1 every year so he has the opportunity to say, "I've played golf every single day this year." If he doesn't play golf on day one, it would be impossible to play every day. He's setting himself up for a streak! If you don't create the streak, the streak doesn't happen. Ever since I heard about Bert's golf goal, I made it my own personal goal to run on January 1.

I have gone running on January 1 for the past five years.

Notice I didn't say I have gone running every single day for the past five years, just that I run every January 1. I run that day because it allows for the rest of the streak to unfold. The year I ran 899 miles, I was terribly ill on January 1, but Dan knew about my streak and how important it was to me. He gathered my running gear, helped me put my shoes on, and ran/walked with me to the end of our block and back. Dan risked a cranky wife because he, too, knew the importance of my streak. Even though I couldn't do much, I did something. And that felt good!

The first step of setting yourself up for a streak is a concrete strategy designed to keep it going. Having a strategy will make it much harder to come up with reasons to skip a day. I was surprised at the number of people invested in my running streak on Facebook. Prior to that, there were a number of followers I didn't interact with much who were runners. When I shared this journey, all of a sudden these like-minded folks emerged and became my biggest cheerleaders.

No matter what, *you* have to do the work. No one else can do that for you. You can't keep a streak going by thought alone. Put in the effort, even if it feels small, and keep going. There's another hidden nugget in the streak— it creates a muscle-like memory for you. You aren't starting from scratch; you are starting with experience. The other day, Caleb asked me to play a very fast piano piece by Bach for his girlfriend. At first I was a bit rusty, and my fingers got tangled on the keys. But then I started playing with ease, and Caleb said, "That was cool. I saw when your muscle memory kicked in." The streaks create the memory of experience, and with that comes confidence. One other thing: when you fuel your soul and start to do amazing things, others will notice and be proud. It shows our friends and family the value of tending to our souls.

Finally, plan something big for the end of your streak—make it special and unique and motivating. Visualize the end with vibrancy. Visualize how you'll feel, what you'll wear, and who will be there. That visualization will keep you going in the middle of your journey, when you might be tempted to lose hope.

> Over the years, running has become my pause. My time to think, to reflect. Running is where the idea of this book first began to take root. As I ran, I started to unpack life, goals, and what it really means to live . . . and an idea was born. This book is a representation of my own soul-spark journey.

## PUSHING YOURSELF

By the end of February in my 899-mile year, I'd settled into a running rhythm and was proud to be thirty miles ahead of my goal. I kept building a buffer of miles, knowing that life happens. At a certain point, Dan wondered if I could push myself a bit more, if the goal was too small. "Do you think you could change your goal to a thousand miles?"

A thousand miles would have felt audacious in January, something completely out of reach when I set the initial 899-mile goal. It felt too risky, too much. But here I was, ahead of my goal and being challenged to up it. Dan could see my hesitation, that fear of commitment popping up. "How much more would you have to run every day, Rach?"

So I did the math. I would have to run 0.3 miles more every day to finish the year with one thousand miles under my feet. It would barely change the time I was gone each day, so I couldn't use time as an excuse. I only needed three more minutes a day (maybe four if I didn't run my typical pace). It didn't change the distance much because I'd run considerably farther in one go. The only thing stopping me from taking the next step was me. I needed three more minutes a day. Let me say that again: three minutes. Okay, maybe four sometimes, but even that is ridiculously small. Upping the goal wasn't an hour more; it was minutes.

This is where appropriate goal setting is critical. When I first began my running journey, this wouldn't have been the goal. You need to be willing to look at your life as it is right now and establish a goal within the context of your starting spot. My starting spot was *not* a thousand miles. Don't judge the start; accept it, knowing that in the future, both you and the goal will reach new levels.

The issue isn't that we can't accomplish our goals; it's that our goals sometimes get distorted to seem as impossible as that claw machine. Some days you will drop . . . but then some days you will feel on top of the world. And this goes beyond running. That was a great deal of my own running story, but I really believe it illuminates the power in pushing beyond goals. Your story will be different, your goals too, but at the heart it is finding yourself, finding your spark, and being willing to set aside the time, make the commitment, and commit to yourself.

What if you wanted to start writing? Could you devote twenty minutes each morning to free writing? Is that possible? By the end of a year, you will have spent 120 hours writing. Can you imagine how much you might learn and grow?

What if you wanted to start your own YouTube channel? Could you invest in a course? Invest the same time as in the writing example above? Imagine how much you would learn and how much happier you could be pursuing something that fuels your spark.

I ultimately decided to add the 0.3 miles to my daily goal, increased my chart, notified my Facebook community, and kept running. My days didn't drastically change, because I was already running. Once a goal is in motion, it becomes easier to pick up momentum because you are already in motion.

One day, while running up the hill to my home, I realized that the cul-de-sac near my house is 0.1 miles long. I decided to tack on that extra tenth, even when I was tired, because I knew that, after ten days, I'd gain a mile without feeling it. What happened next surprised me—instead of just adding the tenth at the end, I started looking for more tenths to add. Maybe I'd run the church loop or the lake trail twice. The tenth became the bonus, the part that kept me realizing I was more than capable of completing the goal.

Once you're in motion as you chase your spark, you'll discover the power of the extra tenth as well.

On December 29, 2022, I busted through a "1,000 Miles" sign in front of my home. It was an amazing feeling, and one I want you to experience as well. And I know you can do it if you set your audacious goal, set yourself up for a winning streak that will keep you going, and then push yourself for that extra tenth. You deserve to do this for yourself!

That extra tenth is grit—it's that commitment to yourself and your capabilities to keep going even if no one sees it. Grit sees the end and thinks, *I can do more*. Grit is found in the single mom working two jobs and attending school online. She's working for a better future and still taking time to fuel her heart. Grit is found in parents sitting in hospital rooms, researching and advocating for cures beyond the given answer. Grit is found in being consistent even when the reward isn't at all close. Grit is fighting for your spark and seeking happiness in a world that might tell you it's a lost cause.

Nurture this gift of a tenth, this 10 percent in your life. It's small but potent. Visualize the 10 percent. Visualize your goal. Work through the steps to make your goal move from safe to going all in. My own little acronym for grit is this: Great Results in Time.

## FIRE STARTERS

+ **Ask yourself, *What if . . . ?*** The best way I've found to push through my own limits is to ask myself, *What if . . . ?* Instead of it being a place where I could fail, *What if . . . ?* becomes *What if I write one more page?* or *What if I run another block?* or *What if I speak up?* The possibilities behind *What if . . . ?* are powerful if you allow yourself to see the positive. One small thing is doable. Your brain might try to convince you otherwise. Or it might even tell you, *You have nothing left to write* or *You are out of stamina* or *People won't like you if you speak up.* Those beliefs are more than likely not true. Doing one small bit extra dilutes the global fallacies ("nothing," "always," "you can't") by proving that you can indeed do just a bit more. You can write, you have the stamina, and you don't need to be friends with those who don't value your voice.

✦ **Recalibrate as needed.** Sometimes life stops your audacious goal in its tracks. My seventy-five-day running streak in 2024 came to a halt when I woke up on day seventy-six with influenza. Even with all the grit in the world, I couldn't run through that splitting headache. If it was life or death, I could have, but it *wasn't* and forcing myself might have been harmful. In that moment, I made a choice: break the streak and care for my body. I was annoyed until I realized this gave me a new target, a new streak to break. If I could run seventy-five days in a row, who's to say I couldn't run seventy-six? Don't let life convince you not to start up again just because of a setback.

✦ **Break things down into small parts.** Smaller parts make the "what ifs?" and the 10-percent-extra possible. You know the saying "How do you eat an elephant? One bite at a time"? The same is true for any goal. In the movie *Apollo 13*, there is a scene where the engineers at NASA are strategizing how to get the astronauts home from their failed lunar landing. At one point, they were trying to make a square air filter fit into a cylindrical hole. No one complained about the lack of resources but instead broke down the steps with the resources they had available. You don't need extra resources either. While the extra resources can make things easier, they aren't critical to success. If you do need more resources, perhaps someone can help you or you can add it to your goals as something you will work toward.

# CHAPTER 10

# WHAT IF I DON'T HAVE ENOUGH MONEY?

## How Rewriting Your Money Story Can Change Your Future

Cathedral Cove, a scenic icon in New Zealand, got its name for the cathedral-like rock structure you can walk through onto the beach. If you've seen *The Chronicles of Narnia: Prince Caspian*, the beach Lucy, Susan, Peter, and Edmund emerge onto from the train is *this* beach. To the east is the vastness of the Pacific, dotted with towering rocks, and behind you rising from the sand is a sheer white vertical rock cliff.

The awe-inspiring splendor can't be captured in photos.

I've been honored to speak in New Zealand a couple times, and both trips have been equally magical. New

Zealand is a glorious, beautiful country, one that grabbed my heart before I'd even crossed the International Date Line. You don't have to be a *Lord of the Rings* lover to love New Zealand, although it adds to the delight. This place has magic in its bones.

On my second visit (I was there to speak about entrepreneurship), we took a day trip to Cathedral Cove. The drive there, like all the drives in New Zealand, was spectacular and filled with luscious green vistas and breathtaking glimpses of the sea. Once there, we trekked a couple kilometers through the forest, down some paths, and onto the beach.

It was magnificent.

I stood there in the white sand, not speaking, and took in the gloriousness of creation. I didn't want to leave, didn't want to walk back through the cove, didn't want to let go of the magical experience.

## 100 THINGS

Twenty years earlier, before my bare feet walked on that iconic beach in New Zealand, I sat in my two-bedroom apartment and dared to write a list: "100 Things to Do in My Life." I was a mom of two at that time and was experiencing some financial issues (not the intensity I'd endure ten years later). My willingness to dream and hope was still there, not doused by defeat. I taped the list on the inside of our apartment door so I would see it every day when I left home. I wanted the reminders as I walked out the door.

When we moved, the list was taped on the wall next to my desk. Not as obvious but still visible. I wanted easy access to it, but I didn't need to see it every time I left home—and I didn't want others to notice the lack of items crossed off. We moved again, this time across the country, to San Diego, where I believed our lives would take a fiscal turn for the better. The list came with me, and instead of next to my desk, I was bold and put it on the fridge. I believed the list might be possible again because I thought my money story was changing. In my head, that meant the list would be attainable and I didn't mind others seeing my dreams. They seemed doable instead of improbable.

Then my world unraveled, crashed down around me, and became a nightmare of severe money drama. The job in San Diego was lost, and we packed up everything, including my list, and drove back to Minnesota. We lived with parents for several months, but nothing was resolved, and for the next ten years, the financial story became a nightmare. In my first book I share the full story and what it took to get out of it—which included bringing my financial distress to light. It meant me sharing my lowest point as well as the grit, mindset, and drive it takes to rewrite your financial narrative. Ever since then, I've been an advocate for financial healing for women, especially when finances are one of the main reasons we stay small and lose our spark.

Just like Grace's fishing lure, my 100 Things list made its way into a keepsake box. But unlike the lure, which represented accomplishment, my list now represented regret and dreams that seemed foolish and impossible. The box sat on a shelf in the top corner of my garage behind boxes of artwork and childhood items, and there it gathered dust.

Several years after my divorce, and months after my New Zealand trip, and after I had been working to actively reclaim my life, I was packing for our move to Nashville. I grabbed the ladder that spring day, climbed up, and started hauling down boxes, many of which hadn't been touched since I moved into the house. That day I found the keepsake box with the list buried inside.

Surrounded by a sea of cardboard boxes, of memories I needed to reconcile (like the box of wedding memories from my first marriage), of stuff I was letting go of and stuff I was bringing, I opened the box. Toward the bottom was that list, folded in half, written by my twenty-three-year-old dreaming soul, "100 Things to Do in My Life."

As I glanced at the list, I took a breath. Number 2 on the list? "Visit Cathedral Cove in New Zealand."

I was shocked. I sat there in the muggy garage as my eyes welled with tears.

If you had asked me to recall what was on the list, I would have said things like "go to Italy" and "write a book" and "buy a house." I wouldn't have remembered Cathedral Cove. But my heart, my soul—they knew. Even though I tried to block out those dreams, my heart remembered. We can try to push away our hopes, can try to tell ourselves they don't matter, but our soul won't forget.

My old money mindset didn't get me to New Zealand. Money is one of those taboo topics, one we're told not to talk about, but unless you can come to grips with your money mindset, your money mindset will have a grip on you.

My money mindset in those years of dysfunction and lack *owned* me.

I used to believe I'd never be able to travel, that the money pit I was in was too deep, that I'd never own a home or be able to fix my credit. In the years since? I've traveled, I own a home, and I've fixed my credit. But it didn't happen overnight. Repairing my finances and reframing my money mindset took many, many years of consistent focus and consistent belief that consistent effort would create change.

I found my 100 Things list in the middle of those life changes, well before I owned a home, and well before my credit was stellar. For me, finding that list in the middle of my journey was like a nudge from the universe, telling me to carry on, that all the hard work would make a difference. When we're in the middle of digging out, those reminders are motivating.

We need a healthy financial story. I know that some of you reading this might be where I was—creditors calling endlessly, counting change in the car, carefully calculating the total in your grocery cart, dreading to open the mailbox to see the latest notice. And some of you might be without worries or fears. It's critical to rightly order your financial story—whether you're dealing with lack or living with abundance. You need to understand your views on money. In some ways, this chapter is one of the most important to me because nothing in my life changed until I changed my mindset about money.

My broken money mindset kept me living under a blanket of shame. That shame smothered my spark. And when our spark is smothered, we can't see opportunities and all our effort feels worthless. We deserve more than to live underneath a belief that does not define our potential.

Let's look at all the different, subtle ways money "truths" make their way into our lives. We're told that money doesn't grow on trees, that the love of money is the root of all evil, that money will burn a hole in your pocket, that money isn't everything, that money is power, and so on. How many of these have informed your approach to your finances? My grandfather, upon meeting people, would often ask, "What do you do to keep the wolf from the door?" My grandfather farmed during the Depression, when money was scarce, and he worked to keep anyone who could take away resources from his door. The question implies that a wolf is out there, and you have to work hard to keep it away from your door, where he could take your money.

Here's where I admit one of my assumptions about money—as a child and young adult I believed *it would just work out*. Remember how no one adds "get divorced" to their yearbook quote? Most of us probably don't add "deal with bankruptcy" or "struggle to make ends meet" either. In my life, because I was wearing the rosy glasses of youth, I didn't anticipate the pressures of not having money, the helplessness that getting behind on payments would bring, the mental toll it would take. I also assumed that money problems didn't happen if you were a good person, and as my money issues deepened, my self-respect dwindled as well.

I don't want money to define your soul, your worth, or your identity. And that's why—get ready—we're going to do a deep dive on money.

## PEELING BACK THE LAYERS

The way we think about money is informed by so much from our upbringing, our culture, our faith community, and our experiences. And those layers go deep. Let's explore.

### The First Layer—Take Responsibility

The first layer I needed to peel back was related to my own money story and my responsibility for where I was. I needed to learn how I got to this place but not get hung up on blame, shame, or worry. Do you remember Ted from *The Lorax*? He was given a charge to move forward. He knew the story of the past, but even with that knowledge, he needed to remove any victim feelings. This layer is fear.

As I began this step, I was plagued by some questions: *What if I don't know what to do to fix this? What if I can't fix it?*

These kinds of questions are what I call *drought mentality thinking.*

Financial fear creates a drought for hope. The drought means you believe resources are slim, there never is enough, and it will be a desperate fight to provide. The drought limits creative thinking because you are focusing on surviving, not on creating stability. Because I had dealt with creditors, liens, and a bankruptcy, I had a deep fear that any money I made could be taken away from me.

Part of accepting responsibility meant acknowledging that I owed money. Even if it was debt from my previous marriage, where I had assumed the role of wife and not breadwinner, and even if I didn't know about them, we incurred those debts together. It would have been easy to get stuck in the idea that I really only owed half. So many people get stuck trying to ensure equity with financial issues, especially after a divorce. Money becomes the stronghold that can not only prevent you from moving on but also halt your healing. I knew that part of neutralizing my relationship with money meant letting go of needing everything to be equitable or fair.

I wanted to be empowered within this responsibility rather than feeling frustration toward my creditors. So instead of seeing those people I needed to repay as a problem, I began to look at them with compassion. I owed them; I needed to repay the debt; I needed to do my part. Fear and drought crowd out responsibility. It also crowds out assertiveness. Once I started to take responsibility, my assertiveness to address my money issues grew. I started making phone calls, and instead of operating from a place of fear, I operated from a place of personal power.

I still had to make sacrifices, be humble, and look for creative solutions as I journeyed down this path. But as I quickly discovered, this mindset was considerably more empowering than allowing myself to feel walked over by what I thought was the enemy. I made phone calls, I shared my situation, and I sought ways to pay my debts. I refused to focus on lack and instead focused on the truth that I could provide.

### The Second Layer—Practice Gratitude

Several years ago, I ran across Ken Honda, a Japanese businessperson who wrote the book *Happy Money*. Honda's money philosophy substantially changed my relationship with money. A big part of that was shifting my mindset to a *relationship* with money rather than simply having a view or perspective of money. We have a relationship with money—a partnership, a give and take, involvement. And in this relationship, money is neutral. It's not evil, ready to show up at your door any moment as a wolf, and it won't burn a hole in your pocket.

Honda asserts that money is energy, the currency of exchange. Honda describes it this way:

> When you approach money with love, you empower it to create positive impact in your life and the lives of others. When you manage it with care, you protect your financial well-being and future. When you share it in friendship, you build meaningful connections and support networks. When you cultivate an abundance mindset, you attract even more opportunities for prosperity. And when you express gratitude for what you have, you open the doors to even greater abundance.[16]

Fear and inaccurate mindsets are what add the negative charge.

If money is energy, then the words you use to describe it are equally important. If you think money is difficult to earn, slips through your fingers, and is always lacking, you are projecting those beliefs onto your life and making them true. Imagine going through life wearing sunglasses that say, "Money is hard to make and keep." Those sunglasses would tint your view so all you see is that belief—rather than realizing that if you take off the sunglasses, suddenly you can see the opportunities.

Honda offers a simple relationship-changing premise regarding money. Say thank you anytime you exchange money (*arigato* in Japanese).[17] When I first read this, it seemed simple enough, so I decided to try it. As I swiped my card at the grocery store, I quietly said to myself, *Arigato*. I received an income check from Google and again thought, "Arigato." Every single transaction, even with those who had put liens on my accounts, was accompanied by "thank you."

Gradually, as I continued this, the exchange of money became an exchange of thanks. Instead of angst and frustration, I was thankful to pay the student loan, thankful to buy that latte, thankful to get paid to speak, thankful to put gas in my car, thankful to pay down my debts. Engaging with my finances was no longer filled with dread but with gratitude.

Money began to change, in my life, from unhappy to, as Honda hoped, happy.

> At the beginning of fixing a money story, there is often a period of working hard at something you don't like. And that's not a bad thing! You're taking back your life, and that requires work. Instead of looking at it as humbling, learn to see it as an opportunity to be empowered. None of us enjoys seasons of penny-pinching or doing nonglamorous work, but when it is done to better your story, it can become a point of pride rather than shame.

### The Third Layer—Rewrite Your Story

As I began to reframe my relationship with money from angsty to happy and as I put in the work to pay debts and earn money, I began to realize I still had deeper hang-ups. I believed that earning money needed to be complicated, hard, and sacrificial. I thought it meant long hours doing something I hated and couldn't possibly be working at something that brought me happiness.

I didn't even recognize this layer until one afternoon with my counselor. "Why do you assume everything related to money is hard?" she asked.

There's that word *assume* again. I told her I didn't know. She didn't buy my quick answer and asked me to think about it more deeply. As I explored my beliefs related to money, I began to realize that I assumed financial peace was hard in part because, for over eighteen years, within my first marriage, any kind of peace or security had felt *impossible*, like the claw machine. My financial situation felt like something I could never fix, that it was hard by its very nature.

"Why does it *need* to be hard?" she asked.

I disliked that question even more. Was it hard because of my capabilities? My past? What was keeping me stuck in the goo of it *needing* to be hard? "Hard is all I know when it comes to money."

Tears rimmed my eyes as the realization hit. I had never lived an adult story where finances were simple, where money was discussed, where financial status wasn't something to be ashamed about. In fact, my entire life had spun a story where money was the archenemy. I assumed I never owned a Cabbage Patch Doll because of money. It might have had nothing to do with finances! I assumed my ex would provide if he loved us enough. But his desire or ability to provide had nothing to do with my worth. I assumed the wolf was coming to my door to take away what I had so I had to always be on guard. But I never even looked to see if there was a wolf to be afraid of.

My counselor kindly looked at me and said with conviction, "Then you need to create a new story."

What story do you want to create related to money, my friend? What is your relationship with money now? And what would you like it to be? If you're in financial crisis, this question may feel like a bitter pill. I've been there. And I'm asking this question from a place of love, as someone who has been there, has been scared out of her mind, and is a friend extending my hand and asking you to trust me. I care about you, and I care about your relationship with money.

Old stories, old debts, old words, old proverbs, old limitations do not need to stop you from writing the most powerful money story for your life! This step goes beyond taking responsibility, beyond thankfulness, and is the core of healing. It's the part of you that realizes you don't have to live like leaves blown in the wind.

You have control over this narrative. You get to rewrite the story. When you rewrite anything, you are starting with something previous and you are making it better, tighter, and more refined. In your money story, start with those beliefs that you might have and begin to reframe them. Pay attention to your response at the store or when you open the mail. Ask yourself, *Is this the response I would have if I lived without money angst?* And then, if it isn't, begin to create the response you, the happy-money-relationship you, would have. You aren't the leaves. You are the wind.

## *The Fourth Layer—Learn Your Triggers*

Triggers are emotional responses to current events based on past events. A trigger will trick the brain into believing a situation from before is happening now. Money stories can have an abundance of triggers. For example, if you've dealt with late bills and lack, imagine you hear a knock at the door . . . Is it a collector? The postman with certified mail to sign? Years later, after the stimuli of the knocks and mail equaling negative, even when you're long past that situation, a knock at the door might still make your heart race. For me, any letter with all caps "IRS" on it is a huge trigger.

The final straw in my first marriage was related to the IRS. I lived terrified of them, gave them even more power than they actually have, and any letter from them used to make me feel helpless. The emotional response of fear at just seeing their letters immediately turned into helplessness.

This trigger has had a stranglehold in my life. A couple months ago, I logged onto my email and checked out USPS Informed Delivery (a service where the post office sends a preview of what mail is coming that day). I have a love-hate relationship with this tool. I love knowing, but knowing what's coming before receiving the actual piece of mail can be so triggering.

As I scrolled through the email, I saw a letter from the IRS. My heart immediately quickened and my palms got sweaty. I noticed that feeling of helplessness creeping in. Ten years had passed since my situation with the IRS was resolved! This response happened when I was sitting in a house I own with a Jeep out front and a pantry stocked with food. But that response was so fast, so instantaneous, so extreme.

I immediately went through the worst cases, the worries, the fears.

And then, because I have been working through triggers, I stopped. Paused. Took a breath.

And then I told myself, "Arigato."

After that, I asked myself one question, which you learned earlier in the book: *If it is the worst case, can you fix it?* And I knew the answer was yes. Could I survive it? Yes. I have survived so much already and could do it again if I had to. So instead of going down the road with that trigger, I reframed my reaction: *Can you wait to have your response until you open the mail?*

How many times do you envision the worst-case scenario before knowing what the scenario actually is? It's easy to do that with money, especially in upside-down stories. Worst-case-scenario thinking robs you of your time now. If I had chosen to spend hours dwelling on the what-ifs of that letter, I would have lost time working and being with my family, because instead of living in the now, I would have been re-creating the past onto the present—and it might not even be true.

Two o'clock rolled around, and as the white USPS truck pulled away, I went out and grabbed the mail. I ripped open the dreaded letter and it said, "Thank you for using the IRS online tool. Please let us know if it wasn't you."

That was it.

Underneath drought thinking, fear, control, and triggers was this worry: I can't solve it. When I saw the letter in my email portal, it unearthed a previous belief of my capabilities. The reason the trigger existed was because I didn't solve it in the past. I relied on others, thought I was getting blown about by circumstances, and lived paralyzed in my own belief system about my capabilities.

I needed to move my belief from past me to current me. The truth is this—even if the IRS letter had been an audit or a bill, it was still solvable. Would that be fun? Nope. Convenient? Definitely not. Would it be annoying? Yes. But would it be solvable? Yes.

What triggers do you have? Are you triggered by an unknown caller? By logging into your bank account? The IRS? Fundraising night at school? Your vehicle with the dent in the door? Asking for help? We *all* have triggers.

The triggers aren't a definition of your worth; they are just the reactions you've developed as a result of challenging experiences. The triggers are an alert. This alert, that quickening of the heart or worst-case-scenario thinking, needs you to catch it. "Not today. Today I refuse to go down that path. No matter what happens, I am confident and capable and will not only get through this but figure out a solution."

Write that out. Speak it out loud. Start to write out your own reframes for your own triggers and claim them loudly. I know you can rewrite your response. Your past beliefs do not have to remain your current beliefs. I believe in you.

### The Fifth Layer—Understand Your Why

In the middle of my son Samuel's seventh-grade year, it became clear that he had impressive abilities when it came to math. He might tell you he's not anything special, but trust me—he's a math whiz. He can understand the steps, and he *remembers* the process. Despite taking calculus in college, I still rely on Google when I try to help him because I don't remember the process.

Samuel also works exceptionally hard. He's never shied away from hard work and puts in the effort to succeed. As a result of his tenacity, near the end of seventh grade, I received an email informing me that Samuel qualified to skip eighth-grade math and go straight to Algebra 1. We had both known it might be a possibility, but when the official invite arrived (and a few "warnings" as well), we both did a happy dance in the kitchen. (Okay, *I* did the happy dance. Samuel stayed middle-school cool.)

The algebra teacher, Ms. Sapp, is known district-wide for her rigorous approach, her commitment to excellence, and her ability to equip kids for the rest of their high school math careers. She assigns a ton of homework and expects the work (and extra) to be completed. Remember the warnings? They weren't just for Sam; they were also for the parents. The warnings were about the quantity of work, the intense expectations, and the truth that they *wouldn't* be skipping eighth-grade math; they'd be required to master eighth-grade math and algebra in the same year.

That first month was eighth-grade math on steroids. It was fast, intense, and quickly weeded out kids who couldn't handle the pressure, adapt, and push through. Samuel, like every student in that class, struggled the first month. Suddenly, my math kid was coming home and telling me how much he hated math. This was the same kid who had aced every single class last year, and even though he was doing what he wanted, he thought he was in over his head.

Because this would happen every year, Ms. Sapp did her best to reassure parents that our high-achieving student who rarely struggled *would* be struggling and that the struggle was good. It wasn't a sign of anything other than being pushed beyond their ease and comfort.

For Samuel and the other kids in Algebra 1, most of school was fairly easy. They knew how to play the game, how to answer the questions, how to do the work, especially the homework. But for many of them, this class was the first time their old strategies didn't work. They couldn't rely on smarts or old patterns but had to be willing to slow down and really examine their methods and strategies.

They needed to understand *why* they were doing *what* they were doing.

When classes were easy, the kids didn't need to understand *why*. But now, every step needed to be explained and understood. Instead of the first layer of thinking, they needed to peel back the proverbial math onion and figure out why they were doing what they were doing.

One night about six weeks in, when I, too, was beginning to question this Algebra 1 decision, Samuel's teacher called to check in. She explained that because most of the kids in this class had never struggled in a class before, the real challenge wasn't the knowledge itself but rather with their definition of self.

For many of them, because academics came easily, they identified as being smart and school was typically easy. So now, when they were struggling, they naturally wondered, *Am I what I thought I was? Am I smart?* Their perception of what it meant to be "smart" was being challenged. Ms. Sapp told me to continue to push Samuel and to reassure him that he was creating a powerful new pattern of thinking.

She had set the bar high because she knew these kids could reach it. This was their opportunity to rise.

One night, while I sat at the table with Samuel as he worked through graphing equations, I messaged my dad about how I was the one helping with algebra now. I also apologized for how incredibly cranky I must have been as a teenager when my dad was helping me. Sam never was cranky, but he was frustrated. I shared his frustration with my dad, and my math-loving, physics-major father texted back, "Tell Sam that I think algebra requires a bit of a mindset change. It's not about getting the correct numerical answer but rather identifying a *method* to get the correct numerical answer. Kind of like the mindset change you must make in chess. You don't win by capturing the king but by trapping the king so he can't escape."

Algebra is about the method, not the solution. It's a shift in thinking.

And that's true with money too. Creating a healthy relationship with money is about the method, not the ultimate outcome.

When I was solely focused on my debts and on how to pay them off, all while shame was stifling me, I was only looking at the solution—become debt-free. The solution felt impossible and light-years away, as if I was climbing out of a gigantic hole. The climb was daunting. Instead of looking at the final destination, I focused on the method and how I was going to climb out. I became creative, patient, and every once in a while, when I'd look up at the desired outcome, I found that I was much closer than before.

If we want to rewrite our money stories, we need to reframe paradigms and refuse to operate out of fear or futility. We need to be willing to look at things differently. When my money situation was at its worst, I remember wondering if someone like the late Steve Jobs, with my resources and in my exact position, could dig his way out. *I knew he could.* I had limited my own possible outcomes and solutions based on old thinking. I needed to dig deep and to change the method.

Sam did the work and focused on understanding the method. Some nights it would take twenty to thirty minutes for one problem, but once he (and I) worked through the strategy, the solution would come.

Work on the strategy, the climb, the steps, and then put in the effort. The solution will come. Sam made it through Algebra 1 not by sitting in his room worrying that it was too much work, was too hard, or might be impossible. He made it through by always focusing on the method and doing the work. I know the same will work for you as well.

## PRACTICAL STEPS

You have the ability to reframe your relationship with money and to make it one of the most productive and powerful partnerships in your life. So how do you do this? How do you start peeling back the layers of thinking behind your relationship with the mighty dollar? Let's take a tactical approach.

1. **Listen to your thoughts about money.** What consistent thoughts run through your mind when it comes to money? Write them down and record the emotions you feel. Maybe you feel guilty spending or you get panicky if your credit cards

are maxed out. As you sit with those emotions, ask yourself, *Why do I feel this way?* The why is where the answer awaits. Don't judge the why. Just write it down. Just like learning algebra wasn't initially easy for Sam, creating new financial patterns isn't always easy. Break down the problem by starting with what you know so you can then figure out the solution. Without understanding how you feel about money, you'll just be guessing at next steps versus clearly identifying the starting point.

2. **Define your baseline.** Once you have a baseline for your money story—whether it's fearful, guilty, neutral, or something else—you need to decide if it's a happy or unhappy story. My money-drought story was clearly unhappy. My story now is happy. You can even write, "I have a happy money story" on stickies and put them around your house. Start Honda's practice of saying "thank you" during a money exchange. When Sam would get really frustrated with algebra, I'd remind him of the excitement he felt about this opportunity. It's all about perspective.

3. **Identify and reframe your triggers.** If being overcharged for something at the grocery store creates anxiety, ask yourself the reason why.

For me, the overcharge wasn't about needing everything to be perfect. It was linked to the fear that I might need that three dollars later. There were times when three dollars made or broke my budget. Just last summer, I waited in line to have my receipt adjusted because I had been overcharged $2.82 on a roast. They were swamped and, in that moment, I thought, *What am I doing? It's less than three dollars.* I decided right then that I was going to stop my obsessive receipt-checking. I would still be smart and look over my receipt, but my time and my emotional energy were worth more than going line by line because I was afraid of losing three dollars. I didn't want to hold on to that fear anymore. Now, instead of being triggered, I simply glance at the receipt, say thank you, and walk out grateful for the food in my cart. Reframing isn't complicated; it just takes commitment and grace.

4. **Remove shame around money.** During the years when I wouldn't talk about money and didn't do anything to change my money story, I was in the worst financial situation of my life. Once I brought light to my money story and faced the issues, I was able to begin reclaiming it. I also

decided to remove shame's emotional charge. A negative charge equals unhappy money. I replaced shame with determination and stigma with pride. And I began to check my mail without being afraid of what I was going to find, because I had taken control of my money story.

5. **Change how you speak about money.** If you say, "It's hard to make money," you are superimposing the qualification of "hard" on your earning potential. Change your words to those that empower: "I am creative and can find many ways to make more than I need." The words you use to describe money will be like a sticky note of truth.

Living with confidence related to money requires making decisions, being convinced of those decisions, and then being willing to change how you look at solutions. It may be difficult to talk about, but money matters. It provides us with opportunities, provides security and growth for our families, and allows us to help others. Do you want to help others? You must have time, resources, knowledge, and life experience to do that—and I know you can succeed in this area. I'm able to share my financial journey and give advice because I've been down this road and come out the other side.

In 2021, I was the keynote speaker for the State of Arkansas Smart Women, Smart Money event. I shared my story, shared about mindset, shared how much I believe in each of the women attending that day. This event led to me being a keynote for the State Financial Officers Annual Meeting, where I was able to share with our state treasurers about financial reform and the need for resources coupled with opportunities. Then I sat on a panel, without shame, and shared my story again—filled with pride that being transparent could help create real change.

All of these things happened because the leader of that group saw me on the *Today* show years before, talking about money. For me, the biggest irony is that money used to hold me back, caused me to hide and live in shame. Now? The place where I felt the smallest has become the place where I speak the loudest.

I see you. I know you can do this. I believe in you. Don't ever let a lack of money be an excuse not to start making changes, and don't let it be a cloak of shame.

As you get healthier, your money story will get healthier.

*Arigato.*

# FIRE STARTERS

✦ **Redefine *hard*—and let yourself try something new.**
We often convince ourselves that things are harder than they really are. Perhaps we want others to be proud of us, so we make sure they know how difficult it was. I have slipped into this martyr-like way of thinking in the past, desperate for others to understand the depths I dealt with each day. You may accomplish things while playing the martyr, but it'll be hard to find happiness and live without angst. Letting go of this challenged my identity. It forced me to reframe my definition of *hard* and reminded me of how much in life is *good* hard—that burn you feel after a workout, the euphoria of finishing a project you've worked so diligently on. Don't make *hard* synonymous with *learning new things*. You can figure out this out!

✦ **Start small.** Take some small steps to see if you can rewrite the story you've told yourself about your ability to make money. Find something in your house you no longer need, take pics, and put it up on Facebook Marketplace or Craigslist. Then wait. There's a great chance someone will exchange money for your item (always be safe, and meet in a public spot). Or try making cards, offer to walk dogs, bake cakes for sale, or sell the tomato plants you started from seed. These small starts could blossom into something more.

+ **Invest in your financial education.** Read books about money, take an investment class, or join a support group. When our kids are teenagers, we take them to an investment class with our financial adviser. Normally, they grumble a bit and wonder why we are making them go, but by the time it's done, they're always fired up (especially about earning a million dollars). And this exercise opens up conversations among all of us about money. I grew up not talking about money and developed irrational fears, so this is incredibly important to me. I know that when we openly talk about money and are grateful—and keep money neutral—everything will be easier. Learning about money boosts your confidence.

# CHAPTER 11

# WHAT IF IT FEELS TOO LATE?

## *Dealing with Age, Dreams, and Time*

My second child, Chloe, has loved cooking, baking, and anything to do with Food Network since I can remember. When she was eleven, she dressed up as a chef from their iconic show *Iron Chef* for Halloween. When people asked what she was, she'd turn slightly, puff her shoulders back, and proudly state, "I'm a chef."

When Chloe turned thirteen, my parents bought her a red KitchenAid mixer, a subscription to *Food Network* magazine, and one of Julia Child's cookbooks. When the movie *Julie and Julia* opened, Chloe and I watched it at least three times. Chloe devoured Child's cookbook, talked about what she was going to make, and set her eyes on one thing—cooking.

Julia Child didn't set out to become a famous chef or television personality. In her younger years, Child was part of an intelligence agency similar to the CIA. She lived in France with her husband, Paul, and while there enrolled at Le Cordon Bleu cooking school. Mind you, this wasn't her first career step. She went back to school when she was thirty-seven years old. She published her world-famous *Mastering the Art of French Cooking* when she was forty-nine. She started her television show, *The French Cook*, when she was fifty-one. And she didn't stop there: she kept creating, advocating, cooking, and inspiring millions, including my daughter, to pick up a whisk and try.

*As a young adult, Chloe wasn't sure what she wanted to do in life. Her "message from the future" moment? The red mixer and the cookbook. Chloe ended up getting a job in a Seattle bakery, then worked the kitchen line, then worked as a sous chef in both Los Angeles and Nashville. Now she's continuing to make a career in the world of food and wine. Even though I could say, "I always knew she could do this," it was Chloe who had the guts to move herself from Minneapolis to Seattle to*

*Los Angeles to Nashville to live out her "Well, maybe I could become a chef."*

My website's inbox receives countless messages asking about age and if it's too late to chase their dreams. Often these women are struggling with feelings of sadness and fear that the time for audacious goals, dreams, trips, and hobbies has passed. I always thank these readers for the bravery to reach out, and then I gently remind them of Julia Child, Bob Ross, and Morgan Freeman—whose careers didn't happen until later in life. But Child? She has a special place in my life because her bold quest to teach cooking created powerful ripples in my own family. Even though so many of us know her story, we forget her ripple and how age wasn't a definer of her future potential.

If age is just a number, why do we still live as if our age defines our options?

Somewhere in our stories, we adopt a belief that we should have figured out life by a certain age. Even though we applaud the Julia Childs of the world, we shrink back and think, *That's for them, not me. What if I don't succeed and I waste the time I have left?* But as we've established, life is a journey of constantly adapting and learning and adapting again, not a static moment of figuring it all out.

Think of it in reverse: imagine someone telling you that whatever you decided to pursue at age twenty-one was the only thing you would ever be able to do. That's absurd!

When you place the labels "I'm too old" or "It's too late to try" onto your spark, your creativity will dwindle. Let's go back to Julia Child, shall we? Prior to learning to become a chef, before being in the intelligence agency, Julia Child went to college to become a writer. She was turned down by *The New Yorker*. And when she decided to write her cookbook, it took nine years to get it published. If Julia had decided at thirty-six she was *too old* to try something new, the dog-eared cookbook on my daughter's kitchen counter wouldn't exist. When we're in a rut or have a setback or feel out of options and proclaim, "I'm too old" or "It's too late to try," our spark inevitably flickers—and maybe even goes dark and just exists as an ember of "what was."

It's riskier to try new things when we're older because we have an awareness that time is finite. It's easy to try soccer, then piano, then dancing, then cooking class when you're a teen. But now—in our thirties, forties, fifties, and beyond—with added layers of responsibilities, cultural norms, opinions of others, and more, it still can feel dangerous to step outside those boxes we're trying to break free from.

What if we fail? What if we embarrass ourselves? What if we're not good at this thing (or it turns out we don't like it after all)? What about what other people might think or say? Any of these things could happen. And people *will* talk. Some friends might think you're having a midlife crisis or that you're being too loud or too risky or simply too much.

Here's the thing: the ways in which people respond is not about you. Whatever you're doing is holding up a mirror to their own life. When you change your story, others see their own story reflected back and sometimes that reflection is uncomfortable. The reflection isn't you: it's the reflection of change, breaking the norm, and stepping outside the box.

When someone's life is full of vitality and their soul's fire is burning brightly, others notice, especially if for years prior it wasn't noticeable. And if their own internal fire is just a flicker, seeing that bright blaze in someone else's life can make them feel discouraged or wonder why their life feels so opposite. So those comments, those questions, they may be less about you and more about them. Instead of feeling judged, step back for a moment and consider, *Maybe something in me is coming alive if I'm getting all these questions.* I ended up using the questions as a motivator and an indicator that I'm on the right track. It doesn't mean you become a jerk and don't listen, but rather you exercise the power of decision-making and decide which comments are empowering or have truth that you should listen to. The rest? Those comments can become residue, so it's best to let them go.

And don't judge people's questions either. Most of them are coming from a place of genuine care and curiosity. Once, on a podcast, the host asked what I'd change about my response during my divorce. That tough question is still in my top five favorite podcast questions. The host didn't assume that I was perfect or a victim of circumstances. He wanted my insight, years later, on what I'd learned and what I would or would not change.

My answer? Have grace for those in your story. During my divorce-fallout years, part of me expected everyone else to immediately adapt to my new story instead of allowing them the grace to catch up, but they didn't have the behind-the-scenes knowledge. They didn't know the nuances, the struggles, and the sheer courage it took for me to flip over the tables of my life. For many, it seemed like Rachel 1.0 one day and then Rachel 2.0 the next day. They didn't know how to fit Rachel 2.0 into their Rachel 1.0 narrative. When my life crumbled unexpectedly, for them, it was as if there was a mirror pointing back at them that made them wonder, *Could this happen to me too?*

That period of life taught me this: change will create ripples. The ripples I felt were varied. Some people left. Some judged me. Some supported me. Some hated me. Some made fun of me. Some helped me. Getting your spark back, fighting for your heart—that will create a ripple, even if you think no one will notice.

Rocks thrown into water will create a ripple that is proportional to the size, shape, weight, and speed at which the rock is thrown.[18] In a way, the big shake-ups in life are much larger rocks or they happen with a great deal more force. And age adds weight to the rock, so when you diverge from a path or jump out of a plane when you're sixty (instead of twenty), you will create a larger ripple of notice.

Any changes will create ripples. And with age, the ripples may seem bigger because people don't expect them. Making waves isn't wrong! Making waves can be inspiring, motivating, and the catalyst for others. Julia Child's ripple is still creating waves, and maybe she'll spark one in your heart too. You might be the same. Your ripple, even if you never see who it touches, might be the inspiration someone else needs to create their own.

Pay attention to the positive feedback, and be gracious while the rest of your world catches up to the new you.

## THAT LITTLE FIRE WITHIN

After my second book, *Mom Enough*, was released, my team put together a rather epic online event celebrating women and motherhood. Over the last decade, Dan and I have established some cool relationships with amazing people: Pat Hazell (a writer for *Seinfeld*), Marja Harmon (star in the Broadway smash *Hamilton*), Alexa Fischer (from *NCIS* and founder of Wishbeads), and dozens more. When we get to meet awesome creatives, we all share our stories, which often includes the question, "How and when did you start?"

Which leads me to my friend Rebecca Lines. Lines is a working actor who recently had roles in *House of Cards*, *Falcon and the Winter Soldier*, and *Cobra Kai*.

Get this: Rebecca didn't become a full-time actress until she was in her forties! Even though she was passionate about her previous career and raising her kids, Rebecca felt this "little fire within" tugging at her.

It wasn't until the middle of the pandemic that Rebecca decided to go all in on making acting a career. Prior to the global shutdown, she was a stay-at-home mom and community volunteer, and she finally got her real estate license once her kids were teens. In 2007–2008, she had just moved to Nashville right as the real estate market crashed. That moment made her wonder if she really wanted to pursue a career in real estate. *Do I love it that much?* she wondered, which led to the question, *What should I do now?*

At first she wasn't sure what the spark was, just that something inside her was craving more. But instead of running from whatever it might be, she leaned in. Then she began to ask herself, *What do I love to do?* She was looking for those message markers, those reminders from our past that hint at our true passions. As she reflected, Rebecca remembered how much acting in high school lit her up inside and how she wished, way back then, that one day she could be a full-time actress. On a whim, she googled "acting in Nashville." She found an acting class, signed up, and was the adult beginner (despite having dabbled for years). That class led to acting gigs, and those gigs led to even more gigs. Then this Realtor-mom was acting alongside Robin Wright, Anthony Makie, Sebastian Star, and Ralph Macchio. And just this winter, she invited us to the screening of *Double Down South*, another movie she's in.

One Google search.
The willingness to be a beginner.
Not letting age hold her back.

Those steps led to the Rebecca I know today, Rebecca the actress.

> *A couple days into 2024, Dan and I met with Rebecca at the Soho Club in Nashville. The Soho Club is for creatives: musicians, actors, designers, and so on. At first, I was intimidated to go, as if I didn't belong. Dan gently reminded me that I, too, am a creative. Make sure to challenge your thought patterns—especially related to age and experience—which can keep you from chasing that fire inside you. Sometimes our old beliefs can stick and others might point them out. Or it might be a hint of our next step—I was fully capable and qualified to be in that room. You wouldn't experience nervousness if you weren't ready to take that step. Shine.*

Have you used age as a reason to stop chasing your dreams? You are no different than Rebecca. What would happen if you let yourself stoke those flames of "Well, maybe I could . . . "? A Google search and taking a risk could lead to more than you ever could have imagined. The only way age wins is if you allow age to speak louder than your heart.

Don't get me wrong; there are some areas of life where we have to deal with the feeling of becoming invisible.

Invisible Woman Syndrome[19] is a documented challenge for women, typically around fifty and/or menopause. During this time, women no longer feel as seen. They feel as if they are overlooked and often ignored. In our world, with externals being so important, this part of aging can be challenging.

But what if we did the work to reclaim this time in life? Even though we know aging is a gift and that each revolution around the sun is a blessing, we still need to deal with the real feelings connected with aging. The wrinkles will happen, the knees will probably creak, and we will get to the point where we might not be "seen" in the same way. And often that's when the feeling of it being too late roars the loudest.

Here are some antidotes:

1. **Create a lifestyle that makes you happy.** Getting your spark back is the first step, but keeping it lit is the lifestyle. You care about your heart. Find the friends to support your heart too. Join a reading or hiking club.

2. **Don't compete.** At least *try* not to. In running, while there is an "overall place winner," most runners only compete with the runners in their age group. I am certainly not trying to beat the

twenty-one-year-old. I'm running to beat my best and compete in my age group. Rebecca Lines is not trying out for a role for a twenty-one-year-old either.

3. **Make the choice to be seen.** Do the audacious things. Write the book. Jump out of the plane. Start the cooking show. Wear what you want. And don't care what others think. Isn't becoming comfortable and proud of who you are the benefit of getting older anyway?

## BACK TO THE ISLAND

Cirie Fields is one of my favorite *Survivor* contestants. She's participated four times, the first time when she was thirty-five. If you're over thirty on *Survivor*, you get put into the older category. These are the contestants who decided not to stay invisible but to put themselves in an environment where they will be seen. Despite the older label, Cirie signed up. She has lived on a *Survivor* island for more than a hundred days and has kept saying yes when *Survivor* asked her to return (multiple times). Cirie kept challenging herself.

During her first season, when she was just the older woman on the show, Cirie told Probst how she used to watch *Survivor*, like a couch potato, but that one day she decided to stop watching and get off the couch and play. She used her age and wisdom to her advantage. She didn't stop, even when she was one of the first voted out. She kept coming back because the adventure fueled her drive. Wondering, *Could I do this?* from the couch turned into the determination to keep playing. On her final season, there was a challenge that took Cirie forever to complete, and despite the other team already winning, she refused to come to the sidelines until she had finished the challenge. Age didn't define her, fitting in didn't stop her—she was a force of nature with a ferociously determined inner drive. Did she have that when she just watched? Probably. But she didn't know it until she allowed it to be reignited.

During her final season, she made it to the final six but became the first player in *Survivor* history to be eliminated not by votes, but rather because every other player had a form of immunity. In the moments before her torch was snuffed, this was the conversation:

"You've played it four times now," said Probst. "You famously got off the couch to see what you were made of. If this is the end of your *Survivor* run, what is the story?"

Cirie responded, "This has been one of the grandest experiences of my life. It changed me. I would have never done any of this if I hadn't gotten off that couch eleven years ago. I would have never met so many different people. I would have never had so many amazing experiences."[20]

I'm going to say it again: she got off the couch.

I don't know how old you are right now, but I want you to know that you do not need to let your age keep you from trying. You can get off the couch. You can listen to the little fires burning in your heart. You can sign up for classes. You can start.

Cirie is now considered one of the greatest *Survivor* players in the franchise. She was forty-six when she ended her last season. Hillary Clinton ran for president when she was sixty-nine. Laura Ingalls Wilder wrote her books when she was sixty-five. Susan B. Anthony founded the International Woman Suffrage Alliance in her eighties. Lucille Ball was forty when *I Love Lucy* first aired. Ariana Huffington started *Huffington Post* when she was fifty-five. Lori Locust was fifty-five when she was hired as the defensive lineman coach for the Tampa Bay Buccaneers. This list could go on and on because, let's face it, we can do great things at any age.

Think about the women in your own life. Who inspires you? Who has pushed back the boundaries? Who embraces aging? They are your people. Listen to their stories, look at the ripples they create, and instead of thinking, *It's too late*, let their courage motivate you to take your own first step.

Make your ripple.

## FIRE STARTERS

+ **Put your wisdom to use.** If you believe that it's too late for you to find your spark, what do you think you were supposed to be doing right now? I can pretty much guarantee it's not sitting on a couch, watching life pass you by. You've experienced a great deal since you were in your twenties. You're wise, you have skills, you care about your future, you want to do your best. Put those years of wisdom to use. What advice would you share with someone just starting? What insight have you gained from the obstacles you've overcome? Just like my financial story has become a place I share wisdom from, you have learned lessons that will help others step into their authentic selves as well. Joan MacDonald is a fitness influencer. She's tough, she can lift heavy things, and she's reclaimed her life. Oh yeah, she started her journey when she was seventy years old. As of this writing, she has almost two million Instagram followers and has graced the cover of *Women's Health.* Her bio? "I inspire others to believe in themselves . . ." What can you inspire women to believe in?

✦ **Be gentle with yourself.** Most of us wrestle with aging. We see the wrinkles, notice the effect of gravity, and then next thing we know, our social media stream and TV commercials are flooded with so-called anti-aging miracles. Those adverts (except for the targeted ones) could have always been there—we just notice them now because their words seem relevant. It's not that I don't want to age; it's more that I'm unsure how to step into the older version of myself. Sometimes I remember a friend from high school who died when she was twenty. She doesn't get the gift of wrinkles, gray hair, and being called "ma'am" at Kroger. I am blessed with that gift. Have you ever seen a picture of yourself when you were younger and thought, *Why did I ever not like how I looked?* If I'm blessed to live to eighty, I suspect I'll look back at pictures of fifty-year-old Rachel and think she looked so young. Be gentle on yourself; the person staring back at you in the mirror needs to love, and advocate, for the person she sees now.

✦ **Do what is right for you.** Social media will present a million different perspectives, and I don't think any of them are "right." Maybe you dye your hair; maybe you're a silver fox. Maybe you love Botox; maybe you use an apple cider vinegar toner and rosemary facewash. The best way I can think of to approach aging is to love others' stories as much as you love your own. Don't criticize others for their choices, and don't buy into the lie that we all need to approach it the same way. So buy the anti-aging cream if you want to! Try the red-light therapy. Buy the walking shoes. Compete in a triathlon. Invest in the "how to dress your best" course. Or don't! But always remember that you are the most beautiful when you love yourself. Love yourself to prioritize doing what you need to do. If you want to get stronger, you are going to have to pick up the weights. Take some time this week to figure out the things you wish you could change or wish you could do and figure out the first step to do them now. You can stop watching life and start playing.

# CHAPTER 12

# WHY CAN'T I DO THIS ON MY OWN?

## The Importance of Fellow Travelers

Growing up in the eighties was an awesome experience. From the arcade at the mall to Nintendo to the first computer my dad bought and taught me to code on, the eighties was when I learned to love technology. One of those memories—beyond Huey Lewis and Prince, pink jelly shoes and Moon Boots, Cabbage Patch Kids and Garbage Pail Kids—was NBC Sunday Night Movie night.[21]

If you were an eighties kid, you might even be humming the trailers that played right before the movie started. Come on, I know you can hear it. And if not, just hop onto YouTube for a bit of nostalgia.

When Sunday night rolled around, my parents would pop popcorn in our trendy air popper with the included butter melting dish into a giant yellow Tupperware bowl. We would drink 7-Up and gather in the lower-level rec room, just us and the movie. No chores, no sneaky "let's fold laundry while we watch" tactics, no agendas. Just us and the tube, rabbit ears ready.

Once a year, the featured movie was *The Wizard of Oz*. This movie was old when I first watched it! It released in 1939, eleven years before my dad was born and thirty-six years before I was born. Our annual viewing of *The Wizard of Oz* is such an iconic experience that my husband, Dan, created an entire episode about the movie's impact on culture on his podcast, *Tracing the Path*.

Until I was ten years old, watching a movie on TV was a synchronous event. You had to carve out the time when it was airing, or you'd miss it. Today there are fewer and fewer synchronous media events because pretty much everything is available online. Sporting events—boxing, the Olympics—or new seasons of network television, election results, movie openers, or the current weather require the viewer to be present when it airs (or you'll soon discover the results in your Facebook feed or on CNN). The VHS changed the necessity to set aside Sunday nights for movies as it gave birth to video rental stores and renting movies to watch whenever you wanted. There's really nothing like NBC Sunday Night Movie today, something that is bound by time and brings all of us together. I've stood in line with my kids for almost all the Marvel and *Star Wars* movies on opening night so they don't experience going to school the next day and hearing what happened. In some ways, that has become my NBC Sunday Night Movie experience with them.

Back to *The Wizard of Oz*. When I was a kid, it kind of creeped me out. I didn't hate it, but parts in the movie made me nervous—flying monkeys, tornados that lift houses, an evil witch with a neon-green face. Remember, I was the girl who believed catching on fire was a possibility, so I'm thinking my childhood line between reality/fantasy and maybe/truth was a bit askew.

My favorite part of our viewing party was when my mom would sing "Somewhere Over the Rainbow" with Dorothy. But as soon as that song was over, I knew I'd be watching Dorothy journey through this crazy world with some dead witch's sparkly ruby slippers on her feet.

As I got older and my reading level increased, as well as library fines for late books, I read *The Wonderful Wizard of Oz* and some of L. Frank Baum's other books. Secret: the books are creepier than the movie! Baum was a magical storyteller and had the ability to weave in nuances about life, friendship, fear, and bravery, but the stories themselves could be unsettling for a child. As the years passed, my appreciation for his writing increased, and I found myself writing papers about him in college and on my blog, even including a section about the Wizard in my first book.

Here's what I think I've learned in my almost fifty years: *The Wizard of Oz* isn't about getting home. It's ultimately about personal power, friends, and the ability to see that they are linked. Yes, Dorothy, who has been transported by a tornado to a magical place called Oz, does want to find her way home, but I don't think that's the heart of the story.

Glinda the Good Witch tells Dorothy she should go see the Wizard if she wants to go home. As Dorothy sets off on the yellow brick road, she makes some friends along the way—the Scarecrow, the Tin Man, and Lion. On their journey, the Wicked Witch of the West sets the Scarecrow on fire, causes trees to come to life and pelt them with apples, and makes Dorothy fall into a deep sleep (creepy, right?). They finally get to Oz, where they encounter the Wizard. But what follows isn't the return ticket home Dorothy had hoped for.

It turns out the Wizard is a fraud.

He's not a wizard at all. He's just a guy from Kansas, hiding behind a curtain and trying to puff up his ego a bit. Despite this revelation, the Wizard presents Dorothy's friends with gifts that symbolize their hopes—a certificate of smartness for the Scarecrow, a heart for the Tin Man, and a badge of courage for the Lion. Then the wizard-turned-man and Dorothy plan to leave Oz in a hot air balloon, but at the last second, after a chance mishap, the Wizard floats away alone, leaving Dorothy stranded in Oz.

This is where the most famous line in the movie occurs. Glinda reappears and meets a distraught Dorothy, crying because all she wanted was to go home. Glinda, in her puffy, glittery dress, looks at Dorothy and says the now iconic line: "You've always had the power, my dear. You just had to learn it for yourself."

Then Dorothy taps her ruby slippers together three times while repeating, "There's no place like home," and wakes up in Kansas.

Glinda's statement is so powerful. I've seen it on posters and prints at bookstores, on shirts, and on Facebook memes. That line is what it means to be human: "You have the power, my dear. You just need to learn it."

We've already explored the power of rediscovering your heart, doing hard things, dealing with aging, and rightly ordering our money. It's time to discover why part of our power involves friendships.

And Dorothy's power came in ways she might not have expected. This wasn't just Dorothy's journey; it was a journey set within the context of friendship. Unlike the movie *Castaway*, where the protagonist's battle is with himself stranded on a deserted island, Dorothy and her friends are in this together. They help each other, protect each other, rely on each other, encourage each other, and support each other. Baum cleverly weaved together each character's journey of self-discovery as they discovered their individual strengths—strengths that once felt like weaknesses—together.

Each character came to the yellow brick road with what was perceived to be a flaw. By the end of the adventure, those "flaws" had been revealed to be strengths—the gifts from the Wizard weren't something they earned but rather a reward for something they already possessed. These friends linked arms and continued the journey together. Think about the friends you have now and those you've had in the past. If iron really sharpens iron, what are ways your friendship has made you stronger? Dorothy made a team of friends, each possessing a skill that made them stronger together.

When Dorothy landed in Oz, she was alone. Yes, she had friends at home, but this journey in Oz was new. She made friends who wanted to walk with her where she was *now*—on an adventure she never anticipated. We have similar experiences in life. There are times when your existing friends might not be present on a new portion of your journey. Just as life ebbs and flows, friendships do the same. And in these seasons, it is a gift when new comrades join us on the journey.

But sometimes when we take a new path and lose the friends from before, we can start to think, *Maybe I can do this by myself.* And yes, there are times in life when you need to do the hard things alone. But there are also times when you need friends. Don't let losing friends or growing apart stop you from daring to make new friends.

My friends from before my divorce—Lori and Maria—aren't going anywhere. But my life changes have brought new friends into my circle—Heather, Cathy, Jason, Tonia, Erica, and Catherine—in this next chapter of life. They didn't just show up on my doorstep either. I had to step off *my* doorstep (or get off the couch) and into situations where I could meet new friends and cheerleaders for the journey.

My friend Catherine and I met three years ago at a Tuesday night meditation class. For more than a year, we'd see each other at class, chat for a bit after, and say, "See you next week." Then one day, Catherine invited me to lunch. We chatted for several hours while eating

Greek food and drinking glasses of iced tea. That lunch turned into another lunch and then another, and the day I stepped into the cryofreeze chamber I mentioned in chapter 3, she joined me.

Friendship takes time to grow. It takes being brave and opening yourself up to new opportunities. It takes walking the road of life with arms linked and being willing to share both vulnerabilities and triumphs. And sometimes all it takes to start something beautiful is one person saying, "Would you like to meet for lunch?"

## YOU HAVE THE POWER, MY DEAR

Successful individuals rarely become who they are on their own. They have friends, teams, comrades, people who believe in them when they doubt themselves, people who are willing to say, "You have the power!" Friends see your strengths and remind you of them and push you to use them. They celebrate your successes and cheer with all their might as you cross finish lines. They sit in courtrooms, hospital rooms, and across the table at Starbucks. They keep us believing, keep us walking down the road even when we don't see the way out. They know that being a friend means being empathetic and sometimes not needing to say anything but rather just being there.

Friends call us out on our BS too. They are willing to say the hard things, even if it means putting themselves on the line. They will tell you when you are making a mistake or are being stubborn. It can get tricky to discern in those moments whether what they are saying has truth in it or if it needs to be let go. But those friends who risk the friendship by speaking up? They are priceless truthtellers.

If you've had a friend challenge you on something, take a minute to appreciate the courage it took to speak up. That person ignored the uncomfortable because she loves you. There are times when I don't want to talk to my kids about changing something, but I know most of the time they'll get over it. Speaking up in a friendship (or relationship) is risky because the other person could decide they disagree and end the friendship. Instead of thinking, *Who does she think she is?* what if deep down you reminded yourself, *She is my friend. She wants good things for me.*

Not finishing college has been a source of shame and embarrassment in my life, similar to my money issues. I went to college for five years and have more than enough credits to graduate, but I don't have enough in my back-then major, architecture. I dropped out after my second daughter, Chloe, was born, and I was determined to go back.

I never did.

I didn't tell many people about this because I thought I'd be judged. Not graduating weighed on me, crushed my sense of self and my sense of pride. It made me feel like an imposter as my success happened.

Then I started writing, sharing my heart, which evolved into a business. The coding skills I had learned in front of a Texas Instrument computer came full circle as I taught myself how to code my website. I kept learning, kept investing in myself, kept figuring things out. Yet I still carried the stigma of not measuring up because I didn't have a "needed" degree. In a way, I subconsciously made this my own bar I "couldn't" get over, my limit in life.

My husband, Dan, before we were married, called me out on my imposter feelings related to that. He said I was holding myself back, longing for a sheet of paper to give me value, and that I needed to examine what I had created instead. He told me that being an entrepreneur means doing things outside the box, being creative, and being daring—which I had already been doing. True friends don't allow each other to use false humility to lessen our greatness. Friends love when their friends are shining brightly.

He cared enough to tell me to stop believing my own lies. Have you had a friend call you out on your limits?

What is your initial reaction? If you debate their words, perhaps they are words you need to hear. Being a truthteller isn't the easiest role, but it is one of the greatest gifts. As you journey together, a friendship rooted in honesty is what sharpens iron and creates bonds. Just like you need your friends to show up, *you* need to show up too, to be the one who says, "I love you so much that I'm going to say the hard things."

My son Samuel has an enviable memory. He remembers movie lines word for word and not just the most common ones. He remembers Bible stories, history lessons, and conversations the same way. People have often told him how smart he is. "No, no, I'm not," he'd reply. Then they'd tell him again and he'd shrug it off, and the cycle would repeat.

After witnessing this exchange loop one day, I explained to Samuel that by saying he wasn't smart, he might be insulting those who don't have the same abilities. It's like Michael Jordan trying to convince you he isn't really that good at basketball or Steve Jobs minimizing his ability to innovate or President Obama denying his charisma. We all have gifts, and whether they're a giant flame or a flickering candle, we should embrace our gifts instead of making them small. Samuel is smart. It's a gift and what he brings to the world. When he embraces it and says, "Thank you," when others notice it, he allows that part of himself to brighten and grow.

Sometimes we use false humility to lessen part of who we are. It's like covering our face because we're ashamed that it's too bright for others. This humility can be a part of feeling like we're an imposter or that others might discover we aren't who they think we are. Friends can also help us distinguish between insecurities, fears, and feeling like an imposter. Sometimes it isn't false humility when we say, "Nah, that's not true." Sometimes it is a legit feeling of inadequacy.

Friends (or parents) have a unique ability to "catch" dismissive words and to be inquisitive. Is what is being said really true? Or does it make you uncomfortable to accept the compliment? Why are you inclined to dismiss the compliment? Even right now, as I ask these questions, consider the areas in your life where you shy away from compliments or dismiss things as "not a big deal." Become the champion of your big-deal moments, share how you got there, and learn to say, "Thank you."

Your people don't care that you didn't finish college, that you don't feel courageous, or that you don't always have it all together. Your people care about *you*, your heart, and your dreams. Your people will fight for you even when you are unaware.

About three months ago, I opened an email from Middle Tennessee State University. Dan, who years ago told me to be proud that I was an entrepreneur, had contacted them about finally getting my degree through them. They told me they'd love to help me get that diploma. I've sent over my transcript from twenty years ago and have been looking at a course catalog trying to figure out which thirty credits I will take. And then? Then I'll have that graduation moment. That diploma is like the fishing lure. It's a symbol. It's more about what I've done *since* college, not what I was doing after college all those years ago. I couldn't believe Dan had done this, and it felt like a really beautiful full-circle moment.

## GETTING IN THE MUD TOGETHER

My friend Heather is a perfect example of a people finder. When I first met Heather, her home was three doors down from mine. For several years, we had a smile-and-wave "How are you doing?" friendship. It was neighbor friendship, first-date friendship, coworker friendship—no deep commitment. And if time went by, we didn't really notice. It wasn't the kind of friendship where I can show up at your house at 7:00 a.m. and I know you'll open the door.

Heather did something that changed our friendship from acquaintances to yellow-brick-road friends.

Heather didn't keep passing by. She stopped and asked me to join her on this life journey. I didn't see it at first, but she was there, asking how I was, sharing personal stories, showing me glimpses into her life. When I'd go past her house on my morning run, she'd be out with her kids waving me on. One day she asked if I'd be interested in doing a Muddy Princess race with her (a 5K combined with obstacles in, you guessed it, the mud). There is absolutely no way to finish one of these races without getting completely covered in mud.

Heather and I are competitive, get-it-done people. For context, Heather won the TV show *Hell's Kitchen*. The talent and tenacity it takes to get through that competition is emblematic of who she is. If you don't know, *Hell's Kitchen* is a reality cooking competition with Gordon Ramsay where he screams at contestants, smashes their food if he believes it's mediocre, and always expects excellence. And that's Heather—she's tough as nails, feisty, outspoken, and gets stuff done. She's always in the middle of a project, works ridiculously hard, and shows up just as hard for her kids. That tenacity and grit is what made her go from thinking, *I wish I had friends* to deciding to make friendship happen.

So we decided to do the race! We completed every single challenge—but not individually; we worked together. One of us would be on top of a pile of dirt, lying down with our hand extended to pull the other up and out of the mud. We did this over and over as we worked together to navigate the obstacles. It really was the perfect picture of how a true friendship works—being willing to get messy for one another and never apologizing for needing help.

Friends don't apologize for their real; friends love each other for their real. That means houses that aren't perfect, lives that sometimes get messy, kids who don't always behave. Real isn't what you see on Instagram, Facebook, or TikTok. Real is dirty dishes in the sink and crumbs in the van. Friends will stand together and do the dishes, not judge the dishes.

After the Muddy Princess race, Heather and I chatted more often, typically in her garage while her three young boys played. We'd wander around her yard, work in her garden, and in the process, we developed the roots of real friendship. Roots take a bit of time to establish, and friendship is the same. It takes those muddy moments and the light-hearted moments to move you from "How's it going?" to "Hello, *friend!*"

One day, right after New Year's, Heather came over in colorful leggings and midcalf rain boots and stated that we needed to start getting together once a week. She didn't ask; she stated. It was a done deal, and she was only clarifying the details. Instead of talking about spending more time together, Heather made it happen.

Our initial plan? Meet once a week for fifteen minutes minimum, no matter what. It could be in the garage, at Starbucks, on a walk, wherever. It was to be a check-in, a recalibration, and a moment of linking arms. That cold January morning, we made a commitment—to show up for each other. That's it. Simple. Solid.

Heather has a level of confidence I admire. Her ability to articulate what she needs is powerful. In that moment, she knew what she needed and why. She stated exactly what she needed, regardless of my possible rejection. I had never met someone who possessed this unapologetic level of "I'm saying what I need."

We started getting together on Tuesdays. I set an alarm for 9:00 a.m. every Tuesday, and when it went off, I'd put on my shoes and walk down the street. We talked, we shared, we cried, we laughed, we watched *Bluey* with her kids, we drank iced espresso . . . And as the weeks passed, we became *real* friends. Instead of surface niceties, Heather invited me into her real life, and I invited her into mine. Over the course of time, both of us dealt with some hard stuff, and Heather ended up navigating divorce. I doubt she knew about my history prior to us making our weekly commitment, but what a gift to have each other as her life took a heartbreaking turn. As the months passed, we pushed through pain, tears, and letting go.

We dealt with some hard stuff, but because of Heather's daring friendship request, neither of us walked alone. And I needed a friend too.

I just didn't realize it when I said yes to her January morning invite.

Sometimes I can be stubborn and believe I can do everything by myself. But then I end up tripping up on my own shoes. I needed a friend to listen and to call me out on my own self-imposed limitations, to remind me that I was strong and capable. I needed a friend like Heather, who told me to write this book and to stop waiting. Friendship is not only a sharpening of each other's courage but also a mirror to each other's souls. Heather could see where I was stalling, and I could see where she needed a kick. Instead of ignoring each other's truths, we each had the bravery to grab each other's hands and say, "I believe in you. Stop making excuses. You can do hard things. And I will be here for you."

Life is too short to walk this adventure alone. We need people.

You might say you're better off alone or that friendship is too risky. I told myself the same lies about friendships for a long time. I had been hurt by some people I thought were stick-with-you friends while going through my divorce. I thought they were walking the road with me, but it turns out they weren't. I took it personally, as a commentary on me, instead of seeing that their choices reflected their journey. I was hurt and angry, so I tried to walk alone. And then real friends stepped in and said, "Sister, you cannot do this alone."

I already know some of you are like, "Nope! Been there, done that. I'm not risking my trust being broken again." And I understand! It *hurts* to be burned by other people. And it's scary to imagine opening yourself up to pain again. But the potential for deep, meaningful, life-affirming relationships is worth the risk.

## GUILTY BY *GOOD* ASSOCIATION

It's possible you might be thinking, *But I can't find/make/ attract friends.* I know that feeling! It took years, not days or months, for Heather and me to progress from neighbors to friends to "I will sit with you while you sleep after surgery" kind of friends. So let's take off the pressure of *making friends* and instead reframe it to be *putting yourself around people who support who you want to be.* Putting yourself in environments where you'll encounter people with whom you might have similar life philosophies is one step closer to finding a true friend.

The responsibility for finding your people and growing friendships is on you. Either you take the risk and put yourself in environments where you can find your people, or you don't. But if you don't try, you can't tell me that finding friends is hard. It *is* hard, but it's impossible if you don't take that first step.

After my friend Maria went through a traumatic divorce, she joined a divorce support group with others who shared a similar story. She desperately needed people who understood the path she'd been on, the trauma, and would be willing to meet her where she was without judgment. She made an investment in herself by putting herself in that vulnerable spot, sharing her heart and her pain and admitting what she wished she could change. Is there an area in your life where you'd like to experience something similar—to find those people to walk alongside you and tell you, "You can do this! You're strong and capable"? Please consider taking that first step to put yourself out there. This is no different than Cirie deciding to get off the couch—which also led to making friends who she never would have met if she had just watched from the sidelines.

I love to remind my kids that they're a reflection of the five people they hang out with most and to choose their friends wisely. One of the kids, who will remain nameless, got in trouble on the school bus years ago. I don't know the full story, just that someone next to him called someone a bad name. He didn't participate, but he was sitting with the kids who did. "Mom! You can watch the tape. I'm innocent!"

But he *wasn't* innocent, I told him. He got in trouble because he decided to hang around with kids who didn't have his same values and did bad things on the school bus. I told him, "Is that who you want to be? Do you want people to assume that is who you are? Because if you keep going down this path, they will think that's *exactly* who you are—a person who disregards rules and says mean things. Even more, if you keep hanging around these kids, there's a good chance you'll start thinking that acting like an idiot on the bus is funny and you may decide to join them."

We need to be guilty by *good* association, not by bad association. We need to find the people who will stand up for us, who will push us to be our best, and who reflect the values, drive, and kindness we also embody.

Find your people—the people who lift you up, who love your dreams, who want that spark of yours burning brightly. Be like Heather, if needed. Reach out and ask someone to spend time with you. Start a women's group, go to karaoke night, volunteer—just put yourself out there. These friends will be there for you in the good times, the hard times, and everything in between. When the speed bumps in life come—loss, death, and more—these friends will keep you going. They are the ones behind the scenes, showing up, giving, lifting you up when you can't walk the road alone. They will hold you up and tend to your heart, your fire.

And when it's *your* turn to be the strong one, that is what you will do.

Being a good friend means you show up for others as the friend *you need*. Look at the friends in your life and how they've been there for you as your example. And be that friend. Be their cheerleader, their advocate, their biggest fan.

This spring, Heather and I ran a 15K together. I had been training, and Heather encouraged me to try to beat my time. We started the race together, and then each settled into our individual paces. At a certain point (it was an out-and-back race, which means you run 7.5 kilometers one way and turn around and run back the same 7.5 kilometers to the start), I saw Heather running toward me as I had made the turn back toward the start.

She started screaming, cheering, and jumping up and down. "This is exactly what I envisioned! I have been waiting this whole race to see you and cheer you on. Run, my friend, run!"

And I'll say the same to you: run, my friend, run!

## FIRE STARTERS

✦ **Hold space for your friends.** Who in your friend group needs you? And are you the kind of friend you would want or need? Find simple ways to show up, to listen, and to be there. Often it takes releasing your own agenda and realizing that relationship happens in the crevices of busy. This spring, my neighbor and friend Tonia's father died from cancer. It's so hard to know what to do. A week or so after the funeral, Tonia came outside while I was washing our Jeep. I was about halfway done and had just soaped up one side. I almost told her I needed to rinse the car before the soap dried. But then my heart said, *Sit with her and just be.* I put the sponge in the bucket and we sat at the end of my driveway in the sun and talked for almost an hour. Yes, the soap dried and I had to start over, but in the long run did that really matter? I would do it all over again, and I know she would do the same for me. Holding space for friends is a sacred gift. Sometimes it's not about the grand gestures but rather the simple moments. Can you think of moments when others have shown up for you? What if today you took a moment to write thank-you notes or send a message to them? What if instead of needing something in return, today was the day you gave back? Friendship isn't something that happens; it takes work, and many times that little note that says, "I'm grateful for you" can mean so much.

✦ **Put yourself out there.** If you're missing solid friendships in your life, I want you to start finding your people. Get involved in some groups where you might find your people—whether that's at CrossFit, a knitting group, a running club, a *Bridgerton* fan club, or whatever makes your spirit sing. Search Facebook for like-minded groups, or go to your community center and sign up for some classes. Find an organization you are passionate about and volunteer. When you actively put yourself out there, you will meet people, and you might just find a great friend. My bonus son, Alex, constantly puts himself out there and tries new youth groups, activities, and events. As a result, Alex has a large pool of friends in all the areas he loves. Instead of just being alone, he was the initiator of the friendships.

✦ **Pay attention to your aura.** Adult friendships can be hard. We come in with stories and life experiences. Yet there are times when we still have the insecurities of our seventh-grade selves, and that distrust of others can be unconsciously felt by them. As you continue to examine the residue moments in your life, pay attention to any limits you've placed on others and on friendships in general. Are you operating under old paradigms? Work to reframe those paradigms, and dare to be vulnerable.

# CHAPTER 13

# SO WHAT COMES NEXT?

## Following Your Soul Map

In 2007, Randy Pausch, a professor at Carnegie Mellon University, delivered a speech titled "Really Achieving Your Childhood Dreams" as part of their The Last Lecture series.[22] Many colleges and universities have these series where professors share with their students their beliefs and personal insights. Oftentimes students will nominate a professor they'd like to hear from "one last time" before they graduate. Pausch described the series this way: "[Where] professors are asked to consider their demise and ruminate on what matters most to them."

One month before Pausch delivered his Last Lecture, he was diagnosed with terminal pancreatic cancer and given three to six months to live. He died at only forty-seven years old, an age when we'd all agree that his time was cut short. When diagnosed, he was a father to small children and seemingly full of vitality.

Except he knew he was dying—and on a clear timeline.

Randy's words were framed within that context—three to six months. Think about how fast that goes in your own life.

Pausch spoke about the seemingly insurmountable brick-wall moments in life. He didn't share how to avoid them but rather what to do *when* you run into them. Brick walls and speed bumps aren't there to stop you; they're there to see who will keep going. Speed bumps aren't the end. They're giving you an opportunity to decide, "I will keep going."

And Pausch had experience with brick walls. When he was a boy, his family went to Disney, and Randy fell in love with the experience and decided that one day he would work for them. As an adult and professor, he felt he was uber-qualified to be accepted as an Imagineer, only to receive multiple rejections: "Thank you for your interest. We will keep your résumé on file." But he kept applying, kept interviewing, kept trying. He didn't let that dream die. Then one day, he came across a virtual reality opportunity with Disney—the exact field he had been working in. He connected with someone in charge and ended up flying to California to meet with them. He told them he'd be willing to take a sabbatical from his teaching position so he could work with Disney, and finally, after all those years, he became a Disney Imagineer.

It wasn't immediate, nor was it easy. But it was worth continuing to push past the speed bumps.

It's a disservice to your soul to assume you won't hit speed bumps and brick walls again. Some speed bumps—loss, death, financial hardship, family rifts, other unexpected moments—will knock the wind from you and might even cause you to question whether you should keep going. No isn't necessarily the end. No can be, like Pausch shared in this inspiring speech, an invitation to keep on trying. To keep doing.

It changes our relationship with the speed bumps. What if you looked back at the speed bumps and decided to try again? What is on the other side? I encourage you to look at those speed bumps as an invitation to keep trying, a reason to keep the fires of your dreams burning, to keep searching for meaning and nourishing your soul.

## CREATING A SOUL MAP

Around the new year, I'll scour the house for old magazines. This task was easier years ago, before everything was online and it was still common for mailboxes to be stuffed with magazines. Despite my nearly magazine-free home these days, I still can typically find some copies of *Runner's World*, a few college brochures, and some catalogs and local fliers.

Then I grab a piece of posterboard, scissors, and glue sticks, and I'll sit at the table with my AirPods and tune into my favorite Spotify station and create a visual collage I like to call a Soul Map. It's like a vision board—but this isn't a vision board of what I want in the future. Instead it's a vision board of my soul, my heart. It's a snapshot of dreams, hopes, and what matters most.

Since I know my tendency to overthink and over-analyze, I set time limits for myself—twenty minutes to cut out anything that piques my interest, twenty minutes to arrange them on the posterboard, and twenty minutes to glue them down. I go with my gut, my heart. I also don't allow myself to look for new words or images during the arranging portion or to move around what I created during the glueing part because I know a different part of my brain is trying to create an image versus letting the image unfold.

Have you ever had a conversation and afterward thought, *I wish I had said this?* Or maybe you've gone to a counselor and when they ask you how you feel, you hear one thing in your head and don't like it, so you change it?

That's the part of our brain that wants to make sure we look good or seem polished. When you don't change the image in this project, when you trust the process and the creation, you get a glimpse into the very fast and often dismissed voice of your heart.

When I'm done, I'm always—always—shocked by the final results. I'm not shocked because it's perfectly put together, but rather I'm shocked because the words and images that seemed random speak to me so powerfully. Words from different magazines combine with images that don't seem to work together, and yet, for me, there is meaning.

To an outsider, my Soul Map might look like a school project. But for me, a depth of insight lies within that collage. Within the freedom to just do, to just be, to not have an end goal in mind, to allow myself to dream, my soul is able to create a map. This is a map of what I have experienced, where I am now, and what my dreams are. The map isn't a literal A to B to C map but rather pieces of my life connected via word and picture. The map is a visualization of "Who am I?" Random words combine with other random words, which combine with images, and together they reveal dreams, things to let go of, achievements, and hopes.

The very first time I made one of these Soul Maps was in that church group with Patti (I shared about her in chapter 4), during the years when I was daring to break free and find my spark again. To my knowledge, that was also the very first time I dared to give my soul the permission to be free and to reignite. Patti had similar rules as I do now—about not overthinking and over-rearranging. She wanted each of us to trust our instinct. The final product didn't need to look perfect; it was okay for it to be raw, messy, not be immediately understood, and real. I still use Patti's approach, including this year when I once again sat down to make a Soul Map.

On that first Soul Map from 2003, one image toward the bottom confused me until just the last five years. It's an image of a little girl with a bow in her hair standing in the snow and looking inside a window. Beneath that image, I had pasted the words "transform you" and "from the heart." Next to her were three lit candles with the word *creativity*. Above her head—and this part chokes me up—are the words "bring you back to" and "dream maker."

Looking at it all these years later, it hit me: that little girl was me. A dream maker.

She was me, feeling like she was watching the world go by and watching everyone living their dreams. She was me, keeping it all together, watching the game but afraid to join. She was me, creativity waiting to burn and dreams she had denied. She was me, waiting to transform her heart, her story.

I once was the girl who felt as if she was watching everyone else live a good life . . . while she stood in the cold watching. I once was the girl looking at the lives of others, wishing hers could have the same spark. I once was the girl who dared to let her heart have a voice.

I didn't know my future story when I created that collage back in 2003. I didn't know the depths of struggle or the heights of joy I would experience in the next twenty years. I did know this: I wanted my life to have meaning. I wanted happiness. I wanted purpose. I wanted to live without fear. But if I wanted that, I had to step away from the window and step into my life. I had to step away from my own inertia and create momentum.

And now? I'm so grateful for the Rachel all those years ago who had the courage to paste pictures and words onto a page, to let it flow from her heart and wonder what it all meant. I'm grateful for the consistent years of taking one step, and another, and the next one. And I believe this experience also means that twenty years from now, if I'm blessed to have those years, future Rachel will benefit from me continuing to dream, continuing to do the work, continuing to fuel my fire.

And I want the same for you. But you have to decide to not just close this book but to take the first step, and the next, and the next, and the next—until living with that vibrancy becomes your normal, everyday posture toward life.

> Future you needs you to stop waiting.
> Future you needs you to step fully into your life.
> Future you needs you to become the happiest person you can be.
> Future you needs you to be a beginner and to start.
> Future you needs you to love yourself—for the first time or again.

And how do you do that now? Each day, as you take small steps, as you do one small thing, as you listen to your heart, as you allow yourself to be known and supported by those you love, you'll no longer feel quite as lost. You won't be stuck in the mire of "what's the point?" because you will be living it out. You will find others on the journey to walk alongside. You may even find that the greatest gift is in helping others overcome areas where you have been victorious.

My life isn't perfect, but, friends, it is good.

Say that out loud: "My life is good." Let those words fill the air around you. Let them fill your soul. Your life is good, even in the imperfections and challenges, because this is your time, your moment, to live on this orb in the middle of a vast universe, and to say, "Thank goodness I cared enough to try."

If you've read this far and are thinking, *I'm inspired . . . but this isn't my story. This is for other people, for those who have been dealt a better hand of cards*, please stay in the game. The "others"? Those people *are you*. Julia Child, Rebecca Lines, Cirie Fields . . . they are normal humans, just like you and me, people who have dealt with challenges, fears, speed bumps, and less-than-perfect lives. The reason we're inspired by them? Instead of waiting around or thinking something was too hard or being the martyr, they took the cards they were dealt and decided to *do something*.

Instead of a fire hidden, *they* dared to let the world see.

We are so good at marveling at everyone else's potential. We fix their crowns, stand on sidelines cheering as they cross finish lines, attend their poetry readings, celebrate their new jobs, are in awe of their YouTube channel, and love their human spirit.

*It's time to do that for yourself.*

> Your story is worth celebrating.
> You are worth a cheering crowd at the finish line.
> You are worth busting through your own limits.
> You are worth finding contentment in the simple moments of life.
> You are worth waking in the morning and being grateful for a new day.
> You are worth reframing your relationship with money.
> You are worth a solid group of friends who love and support you.
> You are worth letting yourself feel your emotions and process your past.
> You are worth caring about your story.

You are worth all of this, and you're worth it today—now.

## BACK TO THE BEGINNING

One January, about halfway through my journey to reignite my soul, I was walking on our neighborhood trail, wondering about everything I had been learning. The foggy feeling had lessened and with it came clarity, like stars emerging in the sky.

*My soul's fire journey was about me finding my North Star—about finding me—again.*

It was me, unapologetically me.

All the questions I worked through, all the mindsets I reframed, all the impossible now possible things I tried, all the extra tenths—they were the fog lifting. The more I tried, the more I could see that my happiness and sense of worth had gotten smothered living without letting my soul breathe. The only way to discover my North Star was to start walking instead of waiting for it to reemerge. It was the doing, the discovering, the daring, and the confidence to keep going.

Your soul's fire is unique to you, and only you. Even now, as we close, I want you to remember that you can't follow someone else's—you need to discover and follow your own.

It guides you and keeps you in line with who you are created to be.

As I walked another realization hit me: I love to write.

I was running from writing, trying to fit into what everyone thought I should do and could do, and forgetting what I was meant to do. Instead of following my soul, I looked at others and thought their way, since it worked for them, must be the answer. Except my soul kept whispering, "Write, Rachel, write again." Your soul whispers to you too.

That's what this journey is about—it's about you no longer denying you but loving your time on this planet so much that you unapologetically step into you. It will mean that you decide not to live with "if only" as a regret, that you are the beginner, and that you deal with anything that clouds your vision.

The journey isn't the destination. It's about you *on* the journey.

That's the good life.

That day, when my realization hit me, I came home, found Dan, and told him I figured it out—I needed to write again. Maybe he, too, was like my counselor waiting patiently for me to figure it out, or maybe he was relieved, but his words back were simple: "It's time, Rachel, for your next book. Let's get the process started."

## THIS IS ME

Writing a book is a messy experience for my family. Originally, I was going to write "for me," but since I've been completely honest with you, I tend to make the entire process uncomfortable for everyone. Anytime a book contract comes in, my family probably has an emergency meeting filled with logistics on how to handle moody, stressed, living-at-the-table, surviving-on-Starbucks, barely communicative me.

There are days when I'm downright miserable.

Yes, miserable. There are days when I don't know what to write, days when I question if I can write, days when I delete four thousand words and panic, days when I'd rather be outside, days when it feels like it will never be done, and after months of waking up and realizing, "It's book-writing day," the crankiness catches up to me. Then one day, about a month before edits were due, Dan reminded me of that tearful January walk: "Your dream was to be an author, and now even in the thick of it, you are living it out."

He's right.

I'm living my dream, living my Soul Map, following my North Star, living what the collage-making Rachel hadn't even dared yet to put to paper. Living out my Soul Map doesn't mean it will always be easy. Living it out means dealing with brick walls and limitations. Living it out requires I put in the effort even when I'm exhausted. Living it out means I say no to the busy so the work can get done.

If it was easy, it wouldn't be a dream.

Then it would be normal and expected. Dreams take sweat, work, belief when everyone else doubts them, tenacity, grit, not having a clue if you're going the right direction. It's a process of zigs and zags and starting over and wondering, *What on earth am I doing?* Dreams push the boundaries of what you deemed possible and require you to keep on showing up. The process is refining, humbling, and will create ripples.

For the past several months, no one has been able to use our dining room table because it's been covered with papers. My weekends have been spent in front of a computer or writing on papers with Sharpies. And trust me, my kids are wondering when life here will get back to normal.

But get this: they aren't asking me to stop. No one is complaining; no one's telling me it's a ridiculous dream. They're proud of their mom, the author, who sits at the table with paper all over and notes and highlighters and her hair in a messy bun. They'll ask each morning, "How's the book going, Mom?" not because they need me to stop but because they know this is who I am.

I am a writer.

This is me, unapologetically me.

An author.

That spark was always there, from those notebooks my dad wishes he had saved, to the eleven-year-old girl who wrote mini-books, to the twenty-year-old who dared to write dream lists, to the thirtysomething who typed in "Finding Joy" as the name for her blog, to the me now.

*You have always, always, always had your soul's fire within you.*

It's there waiting for you to take the journey and find it. It's there waiting for you to unapologetically declare, "This is me."

Your time will pass by no matter what—the days are long, but the years are short. So I implore of you to grab your time—your messy, imperfect, not-what-you-expected time—and live it alive. This is you now, my friend. Your soul fire is the same as it always has been. Your spark will spread and will leave a mark, and it will inspire others to find their own.

You are worth it.

Grab your torch; dip it into your fire.

Sparks spread.

*You are a fire maker.*

# TAKE THE RISK

M y family loves Pixar movies, and we learned quickly that you want to stick around after the movie ends for the bonus short that follows. Thank you for sticking around for this "bonus short" as well. This story is about a defining moment in my life that I've shared in countless interviews, and I hope it will be an inspiring example of what can happen when we take a risk, lean in to the discomfort, and say yes.

■ ✦ ■

Ah, Haiti . . . how do I begin to describe you?

Haiti is a gloriously beautiful country with equally beautiful people. I've spent two weeks there, on two separate visits, and both times my Haitian friends wished the world could see the beauty of Haiti instead of the negative. The negative is impossible to ignore: the government is overrun by gangs, there's intense violence, and it's now on the "Do Not Travel" list. There is brutal poverty (Haiti is the poorest nation in the Western Hemisphere), not enough jobs, and not enough infrastructure to rebuild after multiple natural disasters, two of them being the 2010 earthquake and the 2016 direct impact by Hurricane Matthew. The enormity of the problems is crushing.

Yet when I visited in 2013 and 2017, once to document a mission trip and the other to find out ways to partner with the people of Haiti, I was inspired by the people's determination *despite* the oppression. I sat in clinics where mothers would walk for hours just to wait in lines for days to see a doctor. You'd think they'd be cranky by the time it was their turn, but it was the opposite—a deep gratitude. There wasn't complaining, grumbling, or agitation. Rather, the families would help each other, watch each other's children, hold babies, and simply show up in the smallest but most powerful ways.

On my first trip, when I documented the behind-the-scenes of a mission trip, I asked my new Haitian friends what they wanted me to share, and every single one had a similar theme: they wished the world wouldn't just see the violence and poverty and focus on the city of

Port-au-Prince. They wanted us to witness the generosity, the kindness, and Haiti's exquisite countryside. My mom always used to tell me not to judge a book by its cover, and that applies for countries too.

I didn't have to look for joy in Haiti; *joy found me* in Haiti.

Now here's where this short story gets interesting. On that first trip, sometime between landing at the airport and the last day, I told my friend Jim, the leader, who had invited me along, that it would be cool to ride a motorcycle.

Despite having traffic laws, no one in Haiti seems to follow a single road rule. The free-for-all driving leads to congested roads with seemingly no sense of order. Most people either walk, bike, hitch a ride on a tap-tap (a brightly painted bus), have a car (which people will hitch a ride onto), or use a motorcycle. Most of the time, the only people maneuvering through the chaos are those on motorcycles.

When I think back, I still can't believe I uttered those words or even *thought* that riding a motorcycle was a good idea, especially because I had never, not even once, ridden a motorcycle before. But somehow some part of me thought it would be a great idea.

Months prior, when I was deciding on a location for my trip, Haiti was on the list, but Jim was a bit leery because it typically wasn't someone's first mission trip choice. People often trek there after completing easier trips. But I knew in my heart that Haiti was the answer.

When you articulate your heart or your fears, you are setting into motion a new direction, a new path. It's important to recognize that part of your story. If I hadn't spoken up, the rest of the story wouldn't have happened. The first part of any journey, a critical tool, is voicing your dreams, voicing your heart, voicing your fears so that the universe can get into gear.

When you keep it inside, it's just a thought. Speaking it is the first part of ownership and action.

Finally, after almost a week spent in mountains and villages, the last night of the trip arrived. We all gathered at the local missionary's home and backyard, aptly called Eden. I don't know what the real garden of Eden looked like beyond the illustrations in Bible storybooks, but this place was lush, green, vibrant, and bursting with fuchsia flowers, towering palms, and nature's best selection of beautiful landscapes. I was content, laughing with my new friends and eating my final Haitian dinner of chicken and fried plantains.

In that peaceful moment, Jim yelled my name and pointed to a motorcycle sitting in the gravel driveway next to the portico. I didn't get it at first. I had actually forgotten about my request. "I found you a motorcycle to ride," he said.

"What do you mean?" I replied.

"Don't you remember?" Jim said. "On that first day when you said you'd like to ride a motorcycle?"

The memory rushed back, and I'm sure my freckled face lost all color.

"I didn't forget, Rachel. I found you a motorcycle."

Fear instantly gripped my heart. I am talking the death-grip vise of *What on earth were you thinking that made you say that, Rachel?* kind of fear.

As you continue on your soul's fire journey, please know that you will absolutely, positively have moments when you think, *What on earth am I doing?* Those moments are gold! They aren't an indicator of being on the wrong track. If you didn't have those thoughts, it would mean you weren't pushing yourself or challenging your own limits and you might be letting fear speak a bit too loudly. When you have those *What am I doing?* thoughts, instead of stepping into that fear and stopping, acknowledge the fear—*Hello, fear. It's nice to hear from you*—and then keep going forward with your plan.

You're stepping toward the bike instead of backing away.

So you don't think I'm totally fearless, I did panic—and in only eleven seconds, my brain went through at least a hundred reasons not to get on that bike.

The first and most obvious was that I had never ridden a motorcycle. I didn't even know how to get on the bike, let alone ride it. The other reasons don't matter because that first one is a doozy. I was a literal motorcycle-riding virgin.

But despite fear, despite part of me internally screaming, *NO, NO, NO!* I walked over to the motorcycle. Pretending to be confident, I flipped my leg over the seat and sat down behind the Haitian driver, Bebe, whom I had met only days before. I tried to pretend I knew what to do as I grabbed his waist, just like I had seen others do on the streets of Port-au-Prince.

Apparently I was holding on wrong because three Haitian men ran up saying, "No!" and moved my hands from his waist to small bars a bit behind me—tiny hand grips behind me. Do you see the picture? Instead of leaning in and relying on Bebe to hold me up, I had to lean back and into the bar and attempt to balance. For the entire ride, I was never 100 percent balanced. I had to be active in keeping my balance the entire time.

Even in that there's a lesson! This life journey is never

about finding balance; *it's about balancing.* If you seek balance as an end result, you'll end up quitting, because the moment you achieve balance will be the moment something happens that puts you off-balance. Balancing is doing; balance is being still. The soul's journey is a journey of balancing.

Bebe started the engine, asked if I was ready, and before I could say yes, the motorcycle lurched forward. It wasn't a gentle, rolling, get-used-to-it-Rachel kind of start. It was fast and immediate. I realized the bike had to go faster than I was comfortable with to stay upright.

And that's the next thing you have to add to your soul's fire knowledge—sometimes you have to move faster than you're comfortable with to create change. If you stay at a slow pace, you might be letting fear keep you back. Think of starting a fire. Once it ignites, there is an obvious flame. It doesn't peter out and then build up—there's no flame and then there's a flame. You need that same energy as you pursue your soul's fire.

As we pulled away, I glanced to the left at the rest of the people watching, and I became acutely aware of how sacred this opportunity was. For you church people, don't argue with my use of the word *sacred.* Instead, let it sink into your soul for a moment. This experience was sacred because I recognized the awesomeness of being alive. It was awe-inspiring, a taste of the good life.

I also was aware that I was the only one who would get to ride the motorcycle that evening. I felt responsible to make the experience matter for everyone, to make it count. Somehow I had this intuition that this was more than *just* a motorcycle ride.

Awareness awakens the senses, and as Bebe drove over the grass to a rocky dirt road, instead of fear, life began to rush through my veins. This was life untethered, without the limitations or bars I so easily impose on myself. My fear lessened (but not my grip on those handles).

We drove along a bumpy and pothole-speckled dirt road with towering trees overhead. Gradually, I began to understand the balancing, the leaning, and I thought I was getting the hang of it. But then I started noticing people coming out and waving and shouting things to Bebe. I asked him what they were yelling, and he laughed and said, "They're yelling because they're afraid the American will fall off."

I laughed, but for a moment I was worried as well. *What if I fall off?*

This is the next thing I need you to remember: others might see you and question this fire-maker life. They might think you're going too fast or that you're way out of your element. And you might be—I certainly was out of mine on that bike near Torbeck, Haiti. Instead of believing that their concerns mean you need to stop, use those concerns to remind you why you're doing it. You are daring. You are trying something new.

I didn't need to prove to them that I could stay on the bike. *I needed to prove it to myself.*

I started to get more comfortable in the uncomfortableness of the ride. I loosened my grip just a bit, and instead of being fearful that I'd fall off, I challenged myself to look around and see. This skill of seeing, of looking around, of being present is just as valuable as the balancing. Your soul's fire requires diligence in seeing and being grateful for your now in the moment. *The present and the future are equally valuable.*

After another five minutes, Bebe stopped the bike and asked, "Do you want to go back or do you want to see the sea?" There was no way I was going back. I needed to see this through, needed to see the sea.

He smiled, revved the engine, and pulled the bike to the left and through a magnificent grove of mango and breadfruit trees. The limbs created a canopy, blocking the light.

And then.

My heart.

From the darkness, there was not only light, but heaven, right here on earth.

It was perfect.

We emerged onto an inky-black sand beach framed on two sides by towering mountains, lush with greenery. The waves crashed onto the shore and retreated into the setting sun's sky, a sky painted with crimson, pinks, and oranges. It was beauty in the purest form.

Tears fell.

It was sacred.

I whispered to Bebe, "I will never forget this moment for the rest of my life."

In that moment, my heart was forever changed. I no longer wanted to go back to living numb and just letting life happen. I wanted to be alive, aware, and not so fearful. That moment, on the other side of fear, was my defining experience of what happens when you say *yes* to yourself and *no* to your fear.

The beach moment is one of my top five memories in life—and a moment that forever shaped my future.

Take the risk.

Don't shy from uncomfortable.

Say yes.

Sometimes on the opposite side of fear is exactly what your soul needs.

The spark.

# NOTES

1. Dr. Seuss, *The Lorax* (New York: Random House Books for Young Readers, 1971), 33.
2. America's Got Talent, "Golden Buzzer: Nightbirde's Original Song Makes Simon Cowell Emotional—America's Got Talent 2021," YouTube video, 7:32, June 8, 2021, https://www.youtube.com/watch?v=CZJvBfoHDk0.
3. Olympics, "Derek Redmond's Emotional Olympic Story—Injury Mid-Race | Barcelona 1992 Olympics," YouTube video, 2:35, https://www.youtube.com/watch?v=t2G8KVzTwfw.
4. Maharishi International University, "Jim Carrey at MIU: Commencement Address at the 2014 Graduation," YouTube video, 26:08, https://www.youtube.com/watch?v=V80-gPkpH6M.
5. *Still: A Michael J. Fox Movie*, directed by Davis Guggenheim (Los Angeles, CA: Concordia Studio, 2023) Apple TV+.
6. https://findingjoy.net.
7. I first encountered this word in Mark Manson, *The Subtle Art of Not Giving a F*ck* (New York: Harper, 2016), Kindle loc. 104.
8. Jeffrey Bolognese, "Both/And Leadership," *Medium*, August 7, 2016, https://medium.com/saseprints/both-and-leadership-d5c1107c60af.
9. *Friends*, "The One Where Phoebe Runs." Season 6, Episode 7. Directed by Gary Halvorson. Written by Shana Goldberg-Meehan. Aired November 11, 1999, on NBC.
10. *Friends*. "The One Where Phoebe Runs."

11. Malcolm Gladwell, *Outliers: The Story of Success* (New York: Back Bay Books, 2008).

12. Patrick Kolb, "How Michael Jordan's Mindset Made Him a Great Competitor," USA Basketball, November 24, 2015, https://www.usab.com/news/2015/11/how-michael-jordans-mindset-made-him-a-great-competitor.

13. Nancy Faber and Randall Faber, *Piano Adventures: Lesson Book, Primer Level* (Ann Arbor, MI: Faber Piano Adventures, 1996).

14. Josh Kaufman, *The First 20 Hours: How to Learn Anything . . . Fast* (New York: Portfolio), 2013.

15. TedX Talks, "The First 20 Hours—How to Learn Anything | Josh Kaufman | TEDxCSU," YouTube video, 19:26, March 14, 2013, https://www.youtube.com/watch?v=5MgBikgcWnY.

16. Ken Honda (@happykenhonda), "Money is more than just currency; it's an energy that can be infused with positivity and purpose," Instagram photo, October 22, 2023, https://www.instagram.com/happykenhonda/p/CytEZjfq8Ho/.

17. Ken Honda, *Happy Money: The Japanese Art of Making Peace with Your Money* (New York: Gallery Books), 2019.

18. "Why Is More Than One Ripple Created When a Rock Is Thrown onto the Still Surface of a Pond?," Stack Exchange, July 25, 2019, https://physics.stackexchange.com/questions/493505/why-is-more-than-one-ripple-created-when-a-rock-is-thrown-onto-the-still-surface.

19. R. Krausz, "The Invisible Woman," *International Journal of Psycho-analysis* 75, no. 1 (1994): 59–72. https://pubmed.ncbi.nlm.nih.gov/8005765/.

20. "Survivor: Game Changers - Cirie's Default Elimination Part 2," YouTube video, December 26, 2020, https://www.youtube.com/watch?v=zse_fHH6L1E.

21. "NBC Sunday Night Movie," Wikipedia, last edited May 6, 2024, https://en.wikipedia.org/wiki/NBC_Sunday_Night_Movie

22. Carnegie Mellon University, "Randy Pausch Last Lecture: Achieving Your Childhood Dreams," YouTube video, 1:16:26, December 20, 2007, https://www.youtube.com/watch?v=ji5_MqicxSo.

# ACKNOWLEDGMENTS

To my husband, Dan: this book is just as much a testimonial of what it means to be not only the greatest husband but also a best friend. I'm so thankful for you and love you to pieces. Here's to many adventures together: traveling the world, helping others, raising kids, graduating kids, a bunch of disc golf, and living out our happy story together. I love you always.

To my son Brennan: thank you for letting me share our raw story. I know your vulnerability will help heal many others and provide deep encouragement. Thank you for your bravery, for your love, and for coming back. I love you.

To my kids: thanks for enduring a mom who writes our story. Thanks for loving me and being the greatest blessings ever. And thanks for taking the trash out, cooking meals, and setting out another cup of coffee (with the perfect amount of creamer in it) when I was writing this book. I am your greatest fan and advocate and love you with all of me.

To my mom and dad: thanks for inspiring me to be my best and for remembering the little parts of my heart that I forgot. Mom, please don't give me a time-out for calling you the OG badass. You know you are. And, Dad, I verified the physics facts within the book, just like you always taught me: "Start with what you know . . ." I love you both.

To my mom- and dad-in-love, also known as Mary and Dave: thanks for supporting me as I continue to write about this crazy phase-two journey in life. Thanks for cheering me up, for the many pizzas you've provided, and for being wonderful. Love you both.

To Jason and Cathy: thanks for becoming our friends and for always providing a project for us to work on. Thanks also for asking about this book and all the support you've given. It's really amazing having unbelievable friends just "two doors down." Wait . . . could that be an amazing trivia night team name? I love you both.

To my friends Heather, Tonia, and Catherine: thanks for pushing me to be a better me. Thanks for being the friends to me that I forgot I needed. I love you guys.

To my friend Maria: thank you for sticking with me and for the weekends when I'd text back, "I'm spending fifteen hours writing and can't talk . . ." and still loving me. You are my hero, you know. Our story is now an OG story of friendship.

To my publisher, the wonderful Dexterity, and the entire team: thank you for supporting me and deciding that this book needed to see the light. You are part of my own get-my-spark-back journey, and I'm grateful you took a chance on me so I could share this with the world.

To my publicity team and Lauren: thank you for representing me with such fierceness. Thank you for wanting this book to reach so many and for fighting to get it in their hands. You are amazing.

To my readers: thanks for walking this journey with me and for celebrating when I decided to finally write this next book. Your encouragement and support over the years is priceless. Your spark matters to me greatly.

*Rachel*

# THE VISUAL JOURNEY

This book is without pictures, although I did my best to try to describe the image behind the scene. I wanted you to see yourself in this journey too. But, if you'd like to see the actual images—the motorcycle-riding me in Haiti, the moment of crossing the thousand-mile marker, or even second grade me without the Cabbage Patch doll—you are invited to my corner of the internet.

On findingjoy.net/visualjourney, you'll find a link to more questions meant to inspire, links to videos and movies I've shared, details for making your own Soul Map, and a free thank-you gift from me.

Take the pictures. Record your awesome. And share it.

# ABOUT RACHEL

Rachel Marie Martin is the author of *The Brave Art of Motherhood* and *Mom Enough*. Her blog, *Finding Joy*, has reached over fifty million page views, and her Facebook page has more than one million followers. A champion for moms, the underdogs, and humanity, Rachel believes in the power each one of us has to make a difference, live with joy, and take risks—and that graciousness and kindness are the ultimate gifts we give one another.

Rachel is a sought-after podcast guest, international speaker, and coach. Her articles have been translated into over twenty-five languages and shared on numerous platforms around the world. She's also the cofounder of Audience Industries, a global marketing and training company for creatives, influencers, writers, and podcasters.

After living in Minnesota for most of her life, Rachel now calls Nashville, Tennessee, home. She's married to Dan R. Morris, and together they share eleven children, a son-in-law, a daughter-in-law, and a rescue dog. In her spare time, Rachel enjoys working in her yard, playing piano, running, and being with those she loves. *Get Your Spark Back* is her third book.

Where to find Rachel:

FindingJoy.net
Facebook.com/findingjoyblog
Instagram.com/finding_joy